The Rapture and Beyond gives t
resource for investigating futu_
ture. As usual Dr. Whitcomb writes with great clarity and conviction. This book will be an excellent study tool for all of us.

Paul N. Benware
Professor of Biblical Studies
Arizona Christian University

This superb, must-read volume fondly reminds me of my invaluable seminary training from Dr. Whitcomb (1971-1981)—both replete with a love for God's Word accompanied by irrefutable biblical documentation.

Richard L. Mayhue
Executive Vice President and Dean
The Masters Seminary

Very well done as always ... I pray it will be used to help many.

Charles C. Ryrie
Theologian, Author

Over fifty years ago, Dr. John Whitcomb and Dr. Henry Morris revolutionized evangelical thinking about earth history in *The Genesis Flood*. Now Dr. Whitcomb looks to the future as he teaches what the Bible says about the rapture of the Church and what follows it. I highly recommend Dr. Whitcomb's forward look at the rapture.

Tommy Ice
Executive Director
Pre-Trib Research Center

The Rapture and Beyond by John C. Whitcomb is a treasure of sound eschatological truth packaged in a readable and engaging text. It is a fresh and sound articulation of, and a thorough and reliable exposition of, dispensational, pretribulational, and premillennial truth—a much-needed book written by an accomplished scholar and accessible to a wide audience. Christians who read this book will be grounded in the blessed truth of the "Blessed Hope."

Kevin Zuber
Professor of Theology
Moody Bible Institute

I am delighted with the publication of this work on biblical prophecy by my beloved seminary teacher of nearly five decades ago. Dr. Whitcomb's teaching and writings continue to solidly ground his students on God's Word, one-fourth of which is on prophecy. This much-needed book is solidly biblical, thoroughly researched, and marvelously comforting for these perilous times.

Paul L. Tan
Author, Teacher
Paul Lee Tan Prophetic Ministries

This book is a monumental correlation of multiplied hundreds of biblical truths and their texts in their contexts. It refreshes and reconfirms my pretribulational, dispensational understanding of Scripture learned in seminary over fifty years ago, much of it under Dr. Whitcomb himself.

Rolland McCune
Former Professor of Systematic Theology
Detroit Baptist Theological Seminary

The Rapture
and
Beyond

God's Amazing Plan for the Church, Israel,

and the Nations

Revised and Enlarged

John C. Whitcomb

THE RAPTURE AND BEYOND
Revised and Enlarged

Kainos Books
Waxhaw, North Carolina
kainosbooks.com

ISBN – 13: 978-0615886770

***

Chapter 5 has been reprinted with slight revisions from *Grace Theological Journal* 2:2 (Fall, 1981), 259-63.

Chapter 6 includes portions adapted from John C. Whitcomb, *Daniel* (Chicago: Moody, 1985) and used by permission of Moody Press.

Chapters 7 and 11 are expansions of articles previously published in Tim LaHaye and Edward Hindson's *The Popular Encyclopedia of Bible Prophecy* (Eugene, OR: Harvest House, 2004), 228-32, 401-4.

Chapter 10 is reprinted with permission from the *Baptist Bulletin*, March/April 2011.

Chapter 12 is a revision of an article published in *Grace Theological Journal* 6.2 (1985), 201-17.

Chapter 13 is reprinted with slight revisions from Kenny Rhodes and Keith Sherlin, eds., *Evangelical Bible Doctrine: Articles in Honor of Dr. Mal Couch* (Modesto, CA: Scofield Seminary Press, 2013) and used by permission.

***

Special thanks to Mrs. Vickie J. Broyles for preparing the indexes.

Contents

Foreword

In 1961 the book entitled *The Genesis Flood* revealed the gifted abilities of John C. Whitcomb in understanding and clearly explaining the content of the Bible. That revelation prompted me to enroll in the doctoral program at Grace Theological Seminary in order to study under this gifted servant of God. His example and teaching have made a significant impact upon my life and ministry.

In the years since, Dr. Whitcomb has continued to study and teach extensive areas of God's Word and to record his conclusions in written form. This present book is a compilation of his conclusions related to the following prophetic subjects: (1) the future removal by rapture of all Church saints; (2) the appearance for evaluation of reward of each Church saint at the judgment seat of Christ; (3) the important biblical distinction between the nation of Israel and the Church; (4) evidence that Christ cannot return this year to establish His kingdom reign; (5) evidence that the seventy "weeks" of Daniel 9 refer to seventy periods of seven years; (6) Antichrist's relationship to Israel during the last seven years; (7) the identification and ministry of the two witnesses of Revelation 11; (8) the biblical teaching that, like circumcision of flesh in Old Testament times, water baptism during the present age is not a means of obtaining spiritual salvation; (9) the distinctive roles of Church saints and the people of Israel during the future reign of Christ over the world; (10) the future role of Egypt in God's plan; (11) reasons the Ezekiel 40–48 description of the millennial temple is to be interpreted literally; (12) the purpose of animal sacrifices during the millennial reign of Christ; (13) the characteristics of Christ's thousand-year reign on earth; and (14) the eternal state that lies beyond the millennial kingdom.

Renald E. Showers
Author and Speaker with
Friends of Israel Gospel Ministry

Preface

The sudden and supernatural rapture of the Church is the "blessed hope" for all born-again Christians! At that moment, we shall see our Lord! And "we know that when He appears, we shall be like Him, because we shall see Him just as He is" (1 John 3:2).

Just before He died for our sins, the Lord Jesus promised us, "I go to prepare a place for you. ... I will come again, and receive you to Myself, that where I am, there you may be also" (John 14:2-3). We will not be disappointed with that "place"!

How will this happen? "The Lord Himself will descend from heaven with a shout ... and the dead in Christ will rise first. Then we who are alive and remain will be caught up ... in the clouds to meet the Lord in the air, and so we shall always be with the Lord. Therefore comfort one another with these words" (1 Thess. 4:16-18).

Without dying, Christians who are still alive at that moment shall be instantly glorified!

Then, we will give an account to Him of all that we have done for Him and through Him since we were saved. This is called the judgment seat of Christ. Some will receive a crown, but not all of us: "Each [Christian] man's work will become evident; for the day will show it because it is to be revealed with fire, and the fire itself [of our thrice-holy God] will test the quality of each man's work. If any man's work ... remains, he will receive a reward [i.e., a crown]. If any man's work [not he himself!] is burned up, he will suffer loss; but he himself will be saved, yet so as through fire" (1 Cor. 3:13-15). Without a sin nature, we will totally agree with our Lord's evaluation of our Christian life – thoughts, motives, words, and deeds. That is how the bride, the Church, will have "made herself ready" for "the marriage supper of the Lamb" just before His glorious second coming, seven years after the rapture (Rev. 19:7-9).

And during those seven years, amazing things will be happening on the earth. The Antichrist will appear, and he will make a seven-year covenant with Israel.

Simultaneously, two witnesses for God will appear in Jerusalem – Elijah and Moses! Millions of Israelis will hear their message and will be saved, including 12,000 from each of the tribes. These 144,000 Jewish witnesses will evangelize all nations (cf. Matt. 24:14), while Antichrist sets up his Abomination of Desolation "in the holy place" of the temple in Jerusalem (Matt. 24:15).

Finally, our Lord will return to earth in great glory and will defeat His enemies at Armageddon in northern Israel (Rev. 19:11-21). At last, the thousand-year kingdom of our Savior will be inaugurated! The prayers of millions of Christians will be answered: "Your kingdom come. Your will be done, on earth as it is in heaven" (Matt. 6:10).

The resurrection/rapture of the Church! The marriage supper of the Lamb! The salvation of Israel! The second coming of Christ! The thousand-year kingdom! The new heavens and the new earth! All eternity with our Savior, the Lord Jesus Christ! What great truths to think about and to share with others while the world around us is being engulfed in spiritual darkness.

It was a missionary to India, Dr. Donald B. Fullerton, who led me to the Savior when I was a godless evolutionist at Princeton University in 1943. And it was a great theologian, Dr. Alva J. McClain, who first taught me the basics of biblical eschatology, beginning in 1948. I thank the Lord upon every remembrance of these two godly men, and for Dr. McClain's outstanding book, *The Greatness of the Kingdom.*[1]

I also take this opportunity to pay tribute to my dear wife, Norma, mother of our six children, who has helped and encouraged me in countless ways in my study, my writing, and my teaching of these precious truths.

---

[1] Alva J. McClain, *The Greatness of the Kingdom: An Inductive Study of the Kingdom of God* (Winona Lake, IN: BMH Books, 2001). This classic work is available from BMH Books (www.bmhbooks.com, 1-800-348-2756).

Part 1

THE DESTINY OF THE CHURCH

1

The Rapture of the Church

The night our Lord was betrayed by Judas Iscariot, He encouraged the remaining eleven disciples with these words: "Let not your heart be troubled; you believe in God, believe also in Me. In My Father's house are many mansions; if *it were* not *so,* I would have told you. I go to prepare a place for you" (John 14:1-2).[1]

Then the Savior made a spectacular promise: "And if I go and prepare a place for you, I will come again and receive you to Myself; that where I am, there you may be also" (John 14:3). The disciples could not have fully understood at that time what the Lord Jesus was referring to. Would it be resurrection from physical death? Yes, this will be part of the event, but every true Jew knew this already (cf. John 11:24: "Martha said to Him, 'I know that he [my brother] will rise again in the resurrection at the last day'"). Would it be entrance into the kingdom at His second coming? No, for He will bring all

---

[1] Scripture quotations in this chapter are from the NKJV.

glorified saints with Him from heaven on that great day (cf. Rev. 19:14).

What our Lord was referring to was much more than bodily resurrection, great though that will be. It will be the glorification of living Christians who will never experience physical death – a "blessed hope" for the true body and bride of Christ, the Church. This is a hope that Israel never shared. It is born-again Christians who are "looking for the blessed hope and glorious appearing of our great God and Savior Jesus Christ" (Titus 2:13).[2]

Unique Characteristics of the Church

While still on the earth, our Lord announced: "I will build My church, and the gates of Hades shall not prevail against it" (Matt. 16:18; cf. 18:17). After His resurrection, the disciples asked Him, "Lord, will You at this time restore the kingdom to Israel?" (Acts 1:6). He did not deny that the long-awaited kingdom will come some day. But He did explain that, for now, a new program would begin: "You shall receive power when the Holy Spirit has come upon you; and you shall be witnesses to Me in Jerusalem, and in all Judea and Samaria, and to the end of the earth" (Acts 1:8). This would happen "not many days from now" – on the Day of Pentecost (cf. Acts 1:5, 9; 2:1), precisely ten days after His ascension to heaven.

What was this new program? It was the Church – the spiritual body and bride of Christ. What was the unique characteristic of this new body? It would consist of people – both Jews and Gentiles – who experience Spirit baptism. As He clearly explained, "John truly baptized with water, but you

---

[2] See Thomas Ice, "The Literal Interpretation of Scripture and the Rapture," in *The Popular Handbook on the Rapture,* ed. Tim LaHaye, Thomas Ice, and Ed Hindson (Eugene, OR: Harvest House, 2001), 193-212.

shall be baptized with the Holy Spirit not many days from now" (Acts 1:5).

From the beginning of the world, people (including Adam and Eve) had been saved by grace through faith in God's Word and were "born again" (cf. John 3:3). The Lord Jesus told Nicodemus that he, being a teacher in Israel, should have known this (John 3:10). But Spirit baptism had never been known, experienced, or even predicted for both Jews and Gentiles in the Old Testament.

As the apostle Paul explained, "By revelation He made known to me the mystery ... which in other ages was not made known to the sons of men, as it has now been revealed by the Spirit to His holy apostles and prophets: that the Gentiles should be fellow heirs [with Jewish believers], of the same body, and partakers of His promise in Christ through the gospel" (Eph. 3:3-6).

The true Church experienced a spectacular beginning – Spirit baptism on the Day of Pentecost, along with audible and visible sign-miracles. And it will experience a spectacular departure from the earth – physical transformation when Christ comes to receive us to Himself. This is the blessed hope – the glorification and rapture (i.e., catching up) of all living Christians to meet the Savior in the air just before the Great Tribulation begins on the earth.[3]

No Rapture Hope for Peter

The last recorded words of the Lord Jesus Christ in the Gospel of John look forward to His second coming: "If I will that he [John] remain till I come, what is that to you [Peter]?" (John 21:23).

---

[3] See chapters 3 and 8 for further analysis of the nature of the true church.

In spite of Peter's denial of Jesus in the courtyard of the high priest (cf. John 18:15-17, 25-27), our Lord graciously restored him to the position of leadership he had temporarily abandoned (John 21:1-19). But He also solemnly affirmed that Peter would die – probably by crucifixion: "'Most assuredly, I say to you, when you were younger, you girded yourself and walked where you wished; but when you are old, you will stretch out your hands, and another will gird you and carry you where you do not wish.' This He spoke, signifying by what death he [Peter] would glorify God" (John 21:18-19).

If Peter had the slightest hope of being raptured to heaven without dying, that hope was now removed (cf. 2 Peter 1:14: "knowing that shortly I must put off my tent, just as our Lord Jesus Christ showed me"). But he asked Jesus about the destiny of his close friend and fellow apostle, John: "But Lord, what about this man?" (John 21:21).[4]

Jesus' answer must have amazed Peter and many other believers: "If I will that he remain till I come, what is that to you?" (John 21:22). What did Jesus mean by this statement? Did he mean that John would never die but would experience the rapture? That is what many thought: "Then this saying went out among the brethren that this disciple [John] would not die. Yet Jesus did not say to him that he would not die, but, 'If I will that he remain till I come, what is that to you?'" (v. 23).

Some sixty years later, the aged apostle John, probably the last survivor of the original Twelve, exiled to the Isle of Patmos, penned these words at the end of the book of Revelation: "He [Jesus; cf. Rev. 1:1] who testifies to these things says,

---

[4] The blessed hope of rapture without dying (cf. 1 Thess. 4:17) could not occur until after Peter died. But the believers in Thessalonica, for example, enjoyed that hope, for the apostle John did not record these words of Jesus until long after the death of Peter.

'Surely I am coming quickly.' Amen. Even so, come, Lord Jesus!" (Rev. 22:20). John was probably praying for Jesus to take him alive to heaven – to be glorified and raptured without dying.

The Church Is Not Israel

Our Lord did not tell us specific details about the rapture. He left that for the apostles, especially Paul, to explain. As we have seen, Paul told us that the Church is very different from Israel. The Church is a divine/human organism – a unique *body* composed of both Gentiles and Jews. The origin, nature, and destiny of the Church "was not made known to the sons of men, as it has now been revealed by the Spirit to His holy apostles and prophets" (Eph. 3:5; cf. Rom. 16:25-26).

The Church has not permanently replaced Israel, for that chosen nation will someday be grafted back into their own "olive tree," whose root is the unconditional Abrahamic covenant (Rom. 11:11-24). Paul was very concerned that this be understood by his readers: "For I do not desire, brethren, that you should be ignorant of this mystery, lest you should be wise in your own opinion, that blindness in part has happened to Israel until the fullness of the Gentiles has come in. And so all Israel will be saved. ... For the gifts and the calling of God are irrevocable" (Rom. 11:25-26, 29).

Israel and the Church do share some wonderful things: (1) salvation by grace alone, (2) through faith alone, (3) based alone upon the merits of Messiah/Christ and His work upon the cross. But the differences are also highly significant: the Church has no visible temple, no special class of priests, no animal sacrifices, no Sabbath law, and no circumcision sign.[5]

---

[5] See chapter 3 for an explanation of these significant differences.

Israel had (and someday again will have) all of these. But the blessed hope of rapture without dying is for the Church, not Israel.

Corinthians and the Rapture

The church Paul (and later Apollos) established in Corinth had a special problem with the doctrine of bodily resurrection. Like all Greeks, they rejected this concept because in the afterlife they wanted to be free at last from all physical limitations. That is why we read of the Athenian philosophers, "When they heard [i.e., from Paul at the Areopagus] of the resurrection of the dead, some mocked" (Acts 17:32).

So Paul, as the apostle to the Gentiles (cf. Gal. 2:7-9), devoted a large section of his first letter to the Corinthians to the nature and reality of Christ's resurrection and the resurrection of all believers (1 Cor. 15:3-56).

But the climax of Paul's entire discussion is the rapture of the Church. He wrote, "Behold, I tell you a mystery [Greek, *mysterion* – something previously unknown but now revealed]: We shall not all sleep [i.e., die], but we shall all be changed – in a moment, in the twinkling of an eye, at the last trumpet. For the trumpet will sound, and the dead will be raised incorruptible, and we shall be changed" (1 Cor. 15:51-52).

Paul's Deep Desire

It is important to note that Paul included himself among those looking for this miraculous, instantaneous, spectacular change: "we shall all be changed!" And what kind of change will this be? "This mortal [body] must put on immortality [i.e., become incapable of dying]" (1 Cor. 15:53).

Even the most victorious Christian today would have to agree with Paul that "we who are in this tent [i.e., mortal body] groan, being burdened, not because we want to be unclothed [dead], but further clothed [glorified], that mortality may be swallowed up by life. Now He who has prepared us for this very thing is God, who also has given us the Spirit as a guarantee [down payment]" (2 Cor. 5:4-5).

It was the apostle Paul who stated that dead Christians are in a "far better" state than living Christians: "For to me, to live is Christ, and to die is gain. But if I live on in the flesh, this will mean fruit from my labor; yet what I shall choose I cannot tell. For I am hard-pressed between the two, having a desire to depart and be with Christ, which is far better" (Phil. 1:21-23). It will not be a loss but a "gain."

It will be "far better" because, for one thing, we will be sinless for the first time in our personal existence. But Paul did not want mere sinlessness. He wanted glorification! He wrote, "For we know that the whole creation groans and labors with birth pangs together until now. Not only that, but we also who have the firstfruits of the Spirit [i.e., born-again Christians], even we ourselves groan within ourselves, eagerly waiting for the adoption, the redemption of our body" (Rom. 8:22-23).

And so the apostle Paul, having experienced regeneration – and by now nearly two thousand years of sinlessness – is still awaiting resurrection and glorification, the redemption of the body.

We are awaiting that too, but with this additional blessed hope: glorification without dying by means of the rapture!

The Glorification of Dead Christians

The most detailed description of the rapture of the Church is found in Paul's first letter to the persecuted Christians he

21

had left in Thessalonica. He wrote this letter from Corinth, where he confronted much confusion about the personal destiny of believers. Some Christians in Thessalonica had already died (perhaps by martyrdom), and the saints there were concerned that their dead loved ones would miss out on the second coming of Christ.

But dead Christians will not be forgotten by God at the Second Coming. In fact, they will be the first humans to experience glorification since the Lord Jesus. Yes, Christ was "the firstfruits." He is the first and only human ever to have been glorified. But "afterward" – nearly two thousand years already – members of His body and bride, namely, "those who are Christ's," will share His glory "at His coming" (1 Cor. 15:23).

Now Paul was emphatic in his letter to the believers in Thessalonica on this one point: Dead Christians will be glorified even before living Christians!

> For this we say to you by the word of the Lord, that we who are alive and remain until the coming of the Lord will by no means precede those who are asleep. For the Lord Himself will descend from heaven with a shout, with the voice of an archangel, and with the trumpet of God. And the dead in Christ will rise first. Then we who are alive and remain shall be caught up together with them in the clouds to meet the Lord in the air. And thus we shall always be with the Lord. Therefore comfort one another with these words. (1 Thess. 4:15-18)

It is fascinating to behold the order in which transformations to glory occur: (1) our Lord first; (2) dead Christians next; (3) living Christians moments later; (4) the two witnesses three and a half years later (Rev. 11:1-12); and (5) tribulation martyrs and all pre-Pentecost saints three and a half years later still, at the second coming of Christ (Dan. 12:1-2; Rev. 20:4). Yes, "each one in his own order (*tagma*)" (1 Cor. 15:23), like a magnificent parade through the ages.

The Rapture of Living Christians

It is the third in this order of transformations that we must carefully examine now. After dead Christians are resurrected – hundreds of millions of them instantaneously all over the world – "then we who are alive and remain shall be caught up together with them in the clouds [perhaps glory clouds] to meet the Lord in the air. And thus we shall always be with the Lord" (1 Thess. 4:17).

Watch that word "caught up." The Greek word chosen by the Holy Spirit is *harpazō*, meaning to snatch away.

> The dead in Christ ... will be the first to share in the glory of his visit. Then the living among whom Paul still hoped to be (cf. 'we') will be suddenly snatched away (*harpagesometha*, 'caught up'; cf. Acts 8:39; 2 Cor. 12:2, 4; Rev. 12:5). This term in Latin, *raptus*, is the source of the popular designation of this event as the 'rapture.' So sudden will it be that Paul likens it to a blinking of the eye (1 Cor. 15:52). In this rapid sequence the living will undergo an immediate change from mortality to immortality (1 Cor. 15:52, 53), after which they will be insusceptible to death.[6]

---

[6] Robert L. Thomas, "1 Thessalonians," in *The Expositor's Bible Commentary*, vol. 11, ed. Frank E. Gaebelein (Grand Rapids: Zondervan, 1978), 279. See

It is frankly impossible to imagine such a spectacular scenario. Hundreds of millions of people will suddenly disappear from the earth – perhaps more than 50 million from China alone! Every single believer, even those who have known the Lord for only a few minutes – like the thief on the cross – will vanish.

It will not be a "partial rapture," with only the most worthy Christians going up. If that is the qualification God requires of us, then none of us can be raptured, for none of us is worthy. "For by grace you have been saved through faith, and that not of yourselves; it is the gift of God, not of works, lest anyone should boast" (Eph. 2:8-9).

Just Before the Rapture

Four astounding things must happen before living Christians are raptured to heaven: (1) "the Lord Himself will descend from heaven with a shout"; (2) "the voice of an archangel" will be heard; (3) "the trumpet of God" will sound; and (4) "the dead in Christ will rise" (1 Thess. 4:16).

First, "the Lord Himself [not a mere angel] will descend from heaven with a shout" (1 Thess. 4:16).

When the Son of God speaks – not to mention shouts – great things happen! Consider the psalmist's words.

> By the word of the LORD the heavens were made,
> And all the host of them by the breath of His mouth. …
>
> For He spoke, and it was done;
> He commanded, and it stood fast. (Ps. 33:6, 9)

---

also Renald Showers, *Maranatha: Our Lord Come!* (Bellmahr, NJ: Friends of Israel, 1995), 12.

One word from the Son of God, and the universe began (cf. John 1:1-3; Col. 1:16). Ask Lazarus what happened when Jesus stood at the entrance of his tomb in Bethany, four days after he had died. "He cried with a loud voice, 'Lazarus, come forth!'" (John 11:43).

Someone has said that if our Lord had not specified Lazarus, every person who had ever died would have risen.

No one knows how many will hear His voice. Will it be the whole human race or only dead and living believers? In John 5:25, 28-29, our Lord explained: "Most assuredly, I say to you, the hour is coming, and now is, when the dead will hear the voice of the Son of God; and those who hear will live. ... Do not marvel at this; for the hour is coming in which all who are in the graves will hear His voice and come forth – those who have done good, to the resurrection of life, and those who have done evil, to the resurrection of condemnation [at the end of the 1,000-year kingdom; cf. 1 Cor. 15:23-24; Rev. 20:5-15]."

Second, "the voice of an archangel" will be heard (1 Thess. 4:16). There is only one archangel in the universe, and his name is Michael. God has appointed him to stand guard over the people of Israel against the attacks of Satan (cf. Dan. 12:1). When the nation rejected its Messiah, God broke it off from the tree of Abrahamic blessing (Rom. 11:17) and grafted in Gentile believers to become part of a new spiritual body, the Church.

Thus, in a significant way, Michael too has been set aside during the Church age. But when the true Church disappears from the earth, Israel once again becomes God's exclusive program for salvation, worship, and service. Michael will be thrilled! We will hear his voice – and forty-two months later he will be empowered by the Lord to cast Satan and his demonic armies out of the third heaven, where he has been accusing God's people for thousands of years (Rev. 12:7-10; cf. Job 1:8-11; 1 Chron. 21:1; Zech. 3:1-2).[7]

Third, "the trumpet of God" will sound (1 Thess. 4:16). Paul also referred to this in 1 Corinthians 15:52 as occurring at the time of the rapture. William MacDonald explains:

> It calls the saints to eternal blessing. It is not to be confused with the seventh trumpet of Revelation 11:15-18, which signals the final outpouring of judgment on the world during the Tribulation. The last trumpet here is the last for the church. The seventh trumpet of Revelation is the last for the unbelieving world (though it is never specifically called the 'last trumpet')."[8]

The Dead in Christ

We have briefly looked at three of the four spectacular things God will do just before the rapture of the Church. The fourth and final event – and what an event this will be – is that all "the dead in Christ will rise" (1 Thess. 4:16).

Who are these people? They are people who have believed in Christ since the Church began nearly two thousand years ago in Jerusalem on the Day of Pentecost (Acts 1–2). They include men, women, and children from many people groups from around the world, speaking many hundreds of languages and representing a vast spectrum of cultures.

Everyone who has died as a little child also will be resurrected, for the Lord made special provision for them. Jesus said, "Take heed that you do not despise one of these

---

[7] Some of Michael's ministries on behalf of ancient Israel are described in Dan. 10:13, 21; 12:1. See also his protection of the body of Moses in Jude 9.

[8] William MacDonald, *Believers Bible Commentary: New Testament* (Wichita: A & O Press, 1989), 854.

little ones, for I say to you that in heaven their angels always see the face of My Father who is in heaven. … Let the little children come to Me, and do not forbid them; for of such is the kingdom of heaven" (Matt. 18:10; 19:14).

This truth was revealed a thousand years earlier to King David, for when his baby boy (by Bathsheba) died, he was comforted with the assurance that he would "go to him" (2 Sam. 12:23). David also knew that a person's life begins at conception (cf. Ps. 51:5). Millions of people who have been killed – aborted – before birth are now in God's heaven.

Enoch and Elijah

No one who ever lived before this generation is alive today. This includes Enoch and Elijah, who disappeared from the earth while still alive, for Jesus said, "No one has ascended [in a glorified body] to heaven" (John 3:13).

Our Savior, of course, is the exception, for He received a glorified body nearly two thousand years ago. "Each one in his own order: Christ the firstfruits, afterward those who are Christ's at His coming" (1 Cor. 15:23).

Thus Enoch, who, like Elijah "was taken away so that he did not see death" (Heb. 11:5), was later placed into the realm of the righteous dead to await resurrection. Temporarily, Elijah appeared alive on the Mount of Transfiguration with Moses (who had died nearly 1,500 years earlier; cf. Deut. 34:5). But he was not resurrected. That will happen forty-two months after the resurrection/rapture of the Church (cf. Rev. 11:11-12). Another forty-two months will elapse before all pre-Pentecost saints and Tribulation martyrs will be raised (cf. Dan. 12:1-2; Rev. 20:4-6) to join all glorified Christians in ruling the world under Christ the Lord.[9]

---

[9] See chapter 7 for a study of Elijah's future ministry to Israel.

The Third Heaven

When the Lord Jesus ascended to heaven, He took with Him the soul-spirits – not the bodies – of all believers who had died from Adam and Eve to John the Baptist. They are no longer in "the lower parts of the earth" (Eph. 4:9) – namely "Paradise" (Luke 23:43), or "Abraham's bosom" (Luke 16:22).

Hear the Apostle Paul on this point.

> Therefore He says:
> "When He ascended on high,
> He led captivity captive,
> And gave gifts to men."
>
> (Now this, "He ascended" – what does it mean but that He also first descended into the lower parts of the earth? He who descended is also the One who ascended far above all the heavens, that He might fill all things.) (Eph. 4:8-10)

Later, Paul stated that he "was caught up to the third heaven … into Paradise and heard inexpressible words, which it is not lawful for a man to utter" (2 Cor. 12:2, 4). Thus Paradise and all who were in it were transferred to the third heaven when the Lord Jesus ascended to that realm ten days before the Day of Pentecost (cf. Acts 1:1-11).

The Dead in Christ – What Are They Doing?

Before Christ, believers were often perplexed by the prospect of death. One of God's great servants, Job, recorded his fear that it would be a realm of permanent nothingness.

> As the cloud disappears and vanishes away,
> So he who goes down to the grave does not come up.
> (Job 7:9)

But later, God illumined his mind to write this.

> For I know that my Redeemer lives,
> And He shall stand at last on the earth;
> And after my skin is destroyed, this I know,
> That in my flesh I shall see God,
> Whom I shall see for myself,
> And my eyes shall behold, and not another.
> How my heart yearns within me! (Job 19:25-27)

Many centuries later, even David, who was "a man after [God's] own heart" (1 Sam. 13:14; cf. Acts 13:22), likewise sank into despair at the prospect of death.

> For in death there is no remembrance of You;
> In the grave who will give You thanks? (Ps. 6:5).

But he, too, was given a more optimistic view.

> As for me, I will see Your face in righteousness;
> I shall be satisfied when I awake in Your likeness. (Ps. 17:15).

Another psalmist wrote,

> Precious in the sight of the LORD
> Is the death of His saints. (Ps. 116:15).

Now, thank God, the prospect for dead believers shines even brighter because of "our Savior Jesus Christ, who has abolished death and brought life and immortality to light through the gospel" (2 Tim. 1:10). "To me," Paul says, "to live is Christ, and to die is gain" (Phil. 1:21). In fact, "to depart and be with Christ ... is far better" (Phil. 1:23).

Dead believers are in a "far better" state than living believers! In fact, they have "gain(ed)" something they never possessed while they were alive. What have they gained? God will show us many things about this someday, but here is a starter: for the first time in their personal existence, they are sinless! While he was still on the earth, the mighty apostle Paul had to confess: "For I know that in me (that is, in my flesh) nothing good dwells; for to will is present with me, but how to perform what is good I do not find. ... O wretched man that I am! Who will deliver me from this body of death? I thank God – through Jesus Christ our Lord!" (Rom. 7:18, 24-25).

So what is Paul doing in heaven now? What are all dead believers doing? They are not working and serving, for they are incomplete without a body. They are resting. "'Blessed are the dead who die in the Lord from now on.' 'Yes,' says the Spirit, 'that they may rest from their labors, and their works follow them'" (Rev. 14:13). They are contemplating the glory of their Savior. That is what our Lord asked for: "Father, I desire that they also whom You gave Me may be with Me where I am, that they may behold My glory which You have given Me; for You loved Me before the foundation of the world" (John 17:24). They are worshipping Him in truth and love (cf. Rev. 4:9-11). They are looking forward to the day of resurrection. As Paul expressed it: "Even we ourselves groan within ourselves, eagerly waiting for the adoption [which is not death but], the redemption of our body [i.e., glorious resurrection]" (Rom. 8:23).

The Exalted Position of Dead Christians

Not because of personal merit, but by reason of God's gracious choice, born-again Christians, members of Christ's body and bride, will be the first humans to experience physical glorification since the Savior arose from the dead. The Lord Jesus explained: "Assuredly, I say to you, among those born of women there has not risen one greater than John the Baptist; but he who is least in the kingdom of heaven [i.e., the Church]

30

is greater than he" (Matt. 11:11). John himself announced, "He who has the bride [i.e., the Church] is the bridegroom; but the friend of the bridegroom [i.e., John the Baptist], who stands and hears him, rejoices greatly because of the bridegroom's voice. Therefore this joy of mine is fulfilled. He must increase, but I must decrease" (John 3:29-30). Not personally, but positionally, Christians occupy the highest level of dignity and privilege of all mankind.

Peter saw this too: "To them [the Old Testament prophets and John the Baptist] it was revealed that, not to themselves, but to us [Christians] they were ministering the things which now have been reported to you through those who have preached the gospel to you by the Holy Spirit sent from heaven – things which angels desire to look into" (1 Peter 1:12).

Yes, amazingly, but certainly, "the dead in Christ will rise first" (1 Thess. 4:16)!

The Resurrection Body

Mere moments after all dead Christians have been gloriously resurrected, all living Christians will be transformed and will "be caught up together with them" – without ever experiencing physical death (1 Thess. 4:17). What a blessed hope!

But what kind of body will we have when we are ushered into the presence of our Lord "in the clouds," even being with Him "in the air" (1 Thess. 4:17)? This is a question that cannot be fully answered this side of heaven. But God has given us a few hints that He intends to be sufficient for now.

First, the absolute certainty of bodily resurrection is a basic teaching of the Bible. From the book of Job more than 4,000 years ago (cf. Job 19:25-27) to the book of Daniel more than

2,500 years ago (cf. Dan. 12:2), the people of God were instructed in this doctrine (see also Ps. 16:9-10; Isa. 26:19).

Tragically, some Jews denied this truth. They were the Sadducees, a small but powerful group of leaders in Israel who dominated the high priesthood and were subservient to the Roman emperor. One day they confronted the Savior and ridiculed the concept of resurrection (Matt. 22:23-33).

Amazingly, He showed them in the Pentateuch – the only portion of the Old Testament they claimed to believe – that this precious truth is clearly implied by what God said to Moses at the burning bush: "I am [not, 'I was'] the God of your father – the God of Abraham, the God of Isaac, and the God of Jacob" (Exod. 3:6).

But what did this statement imply? Our Savior explained: "God is not the God of the dead, but of the living" (Matt. 22:32). To us, this may not be clear at first glance. But "when the multitudes heard this, they were astonished at His teaching." Indeed, "He had silenced the Sadducees" (Matt. 22:33-34).

In God's perspective, therefore, dead believers cannot be dead permanently. Without a body, which is essential to full humanity, they cannot experience God's best. Thus, Abraham, Isaac, and Jacob – and all saints who have died – must be resurrected. Yes, God expects us to understand the valid implications of statements in the Bible, not just the "clear" statements. This can happen only if we carefully compare Scripture with Scripture, taking all the words in proper context (cf. 1 Cor. 2:13). The Bible is its own best interpreter.

But now we must ask, "How are the dead raised up? And with what body do they come?" (1 Cor. 15:35) – because resurrected believers and raptured believers will possess the same kind of body. However, it is very important how and why we ask those questions. If our attitude is one of unbelief and skepticism, God's answer will be shocking: "Foolish one" (1 Cor. 15:36). The church at Corinth was notoriously heretical in both doctrine and practice and had to be confronted harshly at times. This is similar to our Lord's rebuke of the two disciples on the road to Emmaus, when they expressed doubt concerning His resurrection – even after they learned that His tomb was empty. "We were hoping that it was He who was going to redeem Israel" (Luke 24:21), they said. In other words, as far as they were concerned, His death destroyed His claim to be the Messiah. To this our Lord replied harshly but, as always, in loving concern: "O foolish ones, and slow of heart to believe in all that the prophets have spoken! Ought not the Christ to have suffered these things and to enter into His glory?" (Luke 24:25-26).

May we beware of ignoring, neglecting, misinterpreting, or denying His Word on this vital subject. The apostle Paul challenged the unbelieving Jewish king Agrippa, "Why should it be thought incredible by you that God raises the dead?" (Acts 26:8).

The Glorified Bodies of Believers

Paul's reply to the questions asked by the Corinthian church about the resurrection body is highly significant and enlightening. First, the *substance* of that body will be different: "And what you sow [in death, like a seed that is planted], you do not sow that body that shall be, but mere grain – perhaps wheat or some other grain" (1 Cor. 15:37). It is amazing how different is the substance of a stalk of corn from the substance of the tiny kernel that is planted in the ground – from which it came!

On the other hand, the *identity* of the body that is raised or raptured is the same as the nonglorified body from which it came. "But God gives it a body as He pleases, and to each seed its own body" (1 Cor. 15:38). Perhaps we will even have the same fingerprints!

This principle of continued identity in the midst of changing substance can be illustrated quite easily. I have crossed the great Mississippi River many times. It is always the same river, but not one particle of water in that part of the river I crossed is the same even an hour later. As for our human bodies, every molecule that was in me ten years ago has been replaced by another. My identity remains the same, but there is a different substance.

The Glorified Body of Jesus

When the Lord Jesus Christ arose from the dead, His glorified body could pass through the tightly wrapped grave clothes and through the huge stone that blocked the entrance to His tomb and through the door of the room where the apostles were hiding.

> Now as they said these things, Jesus Himself stood in the midst of them, and said to them, "Peace to you." But they were terrified and frightened, and supposed they had seen a spirit. And He said to them, "Why are you troubled? And why do doubts arise in your hearts? Behold My hands and My feet, that it is I Myself. Handle Me and see, for a spirit does not have flesh and bones as you see I have." When He had said this, He showed them His hands and His feet. (Luke 24:36-40)

How amazing were the properties of His resurrection body! Yet there was more. "But while they still did not believe for joy, and marveled, He said to them, 'Have you any food here?' So they gave Him a piece of a broiled fish and some honeycomb. And He took it and ate in their presence" (Luke 24:41-43).

Luke states that during the forty days that elapsed between His resurrection and His ascension to heaven, Jesus "assembled together with" His disciples (Acts 1:4). The word translated "assembled" can literally mean he "ate" with them.

What a wonderful confirmation of His continued identity with His pre-resurrection incarnate state as the God-man. He is still, now and forevermore, totally human as well as totally divine. Yes, today and forever, "in Him dwells all the fullness of the Godhead bodily" (Col. 2:9).

In a similar way, all born-again believers will be glorified, yes, but still human – neither partly angelic nor partly divine but totally and permanently human, yet without sin, sickness, or sorrow.

Resurrection and Corinthian/Greek Philosophy

Why did so many in the church at Corinth have deep doubts about the promise of a resurrection body for believers? The amazing answer is that they did not want a resurrected body! Why not? Because they believed that such a body would be nothing more than what they already had – a weak, often painful, unimpressive thing. After all, they thought, who would really want to live forever in a resuscitated corpse?

Their drastic heresy on the design, function, significance, and destiny of the human body, which they had learned from many Greek thinkers of that day, resulted in perverted views of morality and marriage. Note how Paul had to deal with this in 1 Corinthians 6:15: "Do you not know that your bodies are members of Christ? Shall I then take the members of Christ and make them members of a harlot? Certainly not!"

35

In spite of the fact that we still possess sinful natures, even after being born again – a sad reality that Paul explains in Romans 7:15-25 – the mortal body of the Christian is a divine temple! Paul wrote, "Do you not know that your body is the temple of the Holy Spirit who is in you, whom you have from God, and you are not your own? For you were bought at a price; therefore glorify God in your body and in your spirit, which are God's" (1 Cor. 6:19-20).

> The Corinthian pneumatics' understanding of spirituality had allowed them both a false view of freedom ("everything is permissible") and of the body ("God will destroy it"), from which basis they argued that going to prostitutes is permissible because the body doesn't matter ... [1 Corinthians 6] should forever lay to rest the implicit dualism of so much that has been passed off as Christian, where the body is rejected, subdued, or indulged because it is of no significance for – or is even a hindrance to – "real salvation," which has to do with the "soul" ... The body of the believer is for the Lord because through Christ's resurrection God has set in motion the reality of our own resurrection. This means that the believer's physical body is to be understood as "joined" to Christ's own "body" that was raised from the dead. ... Paul ... is taking over their own theological starting point, namely that they are "spiritual" because they have the Spirit, and redirecting it to include the sanctity of the body. The reality of the indwelling Spirit is now turned against them. They thought the presence of the Spirit meant a nega-

tion of the body; Paul argues the exact opposite: The presence of the Spirit in their present bodily existence is God's affirmation of the body.[10]

Resurrection and the Theory of Evolution

For most Christians in the Western world, it is the theory of evolution, not Greek thinking, that has lowered our respect for the human body and dimmed our expectation of a glorified body. But our Lord Jesus Christ, who created all things (cf. John 1:3; Col. 1:16), told us that we have no physical/genetic relation to the animal kingdom. Our Lord affirmed, "He who made them at the beginning 'made them male and female'" (Matt. 19:4).[11]

We are not left in any doubt about this in Genesis: "And the LORD God formed man of the dust of the ground [not from an animal], and breathed into his nostrils the breath of life; and man became a living being" (Gen. 2:7).

And the first woman? "And the LORD God caused a deep sleep to fall on Adam, and he slept; and He took one of his ribs, and closed up the flesh in its place. Then the rib which the LORD God had taken from man He made into a woman, and He brought her to the man" (Gen. 2:21-22).

Consider this: Planning from all eternity the exact physical form He would assume in His incarnate state, and thus the form He would have in His resurrection, the Son of God designed the body of Adam accordingly.

---

[10] Gordon D. Fee, *The First Epistle to the Corinthians*, NICNT (Grand Rapids: Eerdmans, 1987), 251, 258, 264.

[11] Note that God did not put a soul/spirit into the body of an ape. He created our first parents physically. On the creation of mankind, see John C. Whitcomb, *The Early Earth* (Winona Lake, IN: BMH, 2010), 89-112.

In the womb of Mary, and during the third of a century that followed, Jesus "increased in wisdom and stature, and in favor with God and men" (Luke 2:52). That is what Adam and Eve were created to do – and what we were created to do as well. But no animal can do this! No animal was ever created in God's "image" and "likeness" (Gen. 1:26), and therefore no animal will ever have a resurrection body. The difference is profound and permanent. Thus Greek philosophy and neo-Darwinian evolutionism have this in common: they are totally unbiblical and totally erroneous!

When Will The Rapture Take Place?

Our Lord assured us that it is impossible to date the rapture of the Church: "But of that day and hour no one knows, not even the angels of heaven, but My Father only" (Matt. 24:36; cf. 24:42, 44, 50; Mark 13:32-37).

Amazing! Not even the Savior knew the date of His coming again. During the days of His nonglorified human existence – for a third of a century – our Lord set aside the independent exercise of His divine attributes of greatness (omnipotence, omniscience, and omnipresence), though not His moral attributes (holiness, truth, love, etc.). That is the meaning of Philippians 2:7 and 8: He "made Himself of no reputation ... He humbled Himself and became obedient to the point of death, even the death of the cross."

Over and over again, our LORD explained: "I do nothing of Myself; but as My Father taught Me, I speak these things" (John 8:28); and, "The Father who sent Me gave Me a command, what I should say and what I should speak. ... Therefore, whatever I speak, just as the Father has told Me, so I speak" (John 12:49-50; cf. 5:20; 7:16; 8:38, 40; 15:15; 17:8).

Why did the Father withhold the date of the rapture from His own Son? As we have seen, our Savior temporarily set aside the independent exercise of His own omniscience. But consider carefully where the Lord Jesus placed Himself in this "day-of-His-coming pyramid of ignorance." Bottom level – He knew that "no one [no human being] knows" the timing "of that day and hour" (Mark 13:32). Higher level – He also knew that "not even the angels in heaven" know the time of the rapture. Highest level – Jesus referred to Himself with the words "nor the Son."

Jesus placed Himself above all men and all angels, and He knew that "only the Father" – the Capstone of this "pyramid" – knew the date.[12]

Yes, of course, the Father has always known that day and hour. And since His resurrection, the Son knows when He will come for His bride, the true Church. One thing is certain: it will happen in "the fullness of the time" (Gal. 4:4), not too soon and not too late. That is when His first coming occurred: "When the fullness of the time had come, God sent forth His Son, born of a woman, born under the law" (Gal. 4:4).

There is a significant difference, however. The nation of Israel was told when the first coming of Messiah would take place, namely, 483 years after the decree of King Artaxerxes to rebuild the walls of Jerusalem. That decree was issued in 445 BC (cf. Neh. 2:8; Dan. 9:25). It was probably this prediction that our Lord referred to when He wept over Jerusalem and exclaimed, "If you had known, even you, especially in this your day, the things that make for your peace! But now they are hidden from your eyes" (Luke 19:42).

God has given us no date for the Second Coming, however. The resurrection and rapture of the Church is imminent – it can happen at any moment, night or day. This is

---

12 See chapter 4, especially pages 67-68.

God's very effective way to keep us on the alert. Our Savior stated,

> Watch therefore, for you do not know what hour your Lord is coming. But know this, that if the master of the house had known what hour the thief would come, he would have watched and not allowed his house to be broken into. Therefore you also be ready, for the Son of Man is coming at an hour you do not expect. (Matt. 24:42-44; cf. 24:50; 25:13)

Friend, are you ready to meet the Lord at any moment? Is He truly your personal Savior from the penalty of sin? Have you put your trust in Him for eternal salvation? Is His soon appearing your "blessed hope" (Titus 2:13)? "Establish your hearts, for the coming of the Lord is at hand. ... Behold, the Judge is standing at the door!" (James 5:8-9).

2

The Believer's Heavenly Rewards

All true Christians must surely rejoice at the thought of God's wonderful promise and provision that, "If we confess our sins, He is faithful and just to forgive us our sins and to cleanse us from all unrighteousness" (1 John 1:9).[1]

But how does this divine provision relate to Christ's confrontation with His Church, His body and bride, at the judgment throne? Does participation in the marvelous promise of 1 John 1:9 eliminate the threat of possibly losing a reward or a crown on that great day? This is a very confusing issue for many of God's people today.[2]

The Purpose of the Judgment Seat Confrontation

One point must be settled immediately – the issue is the gain or loss of rewards, not of salvation. Thank God, "He who has begun a good work in you will complete it until the day of Jesus Christ" (Phil. 1:6). And, "having been justified by faith, we have peace with God through our Lord Jesus Christ ... and rejoice in hope of the glory of God" (Rom. 5:1-2).

---

[1] Scripture quotations in this chapter are from the NKJV.

[2] For excellent insights on this complex topic, see Samuel L. Hoyt, *The Judgment Seat of Christ* (Milwaukee: Grace Gospel Press, 2011).

Also, Jesus said, "He who hears My word and believes in Him who sent Me has everlasting life, and shall not come into judgment, but has passed from death into life" (John 5:24). And amazingly, our Lord said this concerning all believers: "I give them eternal life, and they shall never perish ... no one is able to snatch them out of My Father's hand. I and My Father are one" (John 10:28-30).

On the other hand, the provision of awards for faithfulness is intended by our Lord to provide tremendous motivation for His people. As a matter of fact, all human beings have been programmed by God with this perspective. How would a military unit function efficiently and effectively if there were no rewards for self-discipline, diligence, and courage?

Both my grandfather and my father attained high rank in the United States Army and were deeply involved in the Spanish-American War, World War I, and World War II. As a child, I heard much about promotions to higher rank, medals, awards, and special recognition. No army in the world could function without this! And what about governments, industries, and schools? Would a student do his or her very best if there were no grades or honors at the end?

Prizes, Crowns, and Rewards

The apostle Paul was well aware of the prizes offered to athletes who competed at the Isthmian Games of his day. "These Games, held every two years under the patronage of Corinth and second only to the Olympics, were extravagant festivals of religion, athletics, and the arts, attracting thousands of competitors and visitors from all over the empire ...

Paul would have been in Corinth during the games of A.D. 51 (in the spring)."[3]

It was to the church at Corinth that Paul wrote: "Do you not know that those who run in a race all run, but one receives the prize? Run in such a way that you may obtain it. And everyone who competes for the prize is temperate in all things. Now they do it to obtain a perishable crown, but we for an imperishable *crown*. Therefore I run thus: not with uncertainty. Thus I fight: not as one who beats the air. But I discipline my body and bring it into subjection, lest, when I have preached to others, I myself should become disqualified" (1 Cor. 9:24-27).

Sadly, a very popular version of the Bible mistranslated that word "disqualified" [*adokimos*] as "castaway," implying loss of salvation. Lewis Sperry Chafer helpfully explained, "It is the negative form, and its positive is rightly translated in 2 Timothy 2:15, 'Study to show thyself approved [dokimos] unto God.' The disapproval which the Apostle dreaded is none other than the burning of unworthy works of service (cf. 2 Cor. 5:11)."[4]

Paul also warned the church at Colosse: "Let no one cheat you of your reward" (Col. 2:18).

In spite of having a sin nature like all of us, the apostle Paul struggled valiantly, through Christ ("I do not count myself to have apprehended; but ... I press toward the goal for the prize of the upward call of God in Christ Jesus" [Phil. 3:13-

---

[3] Gordon D. Fee, *The First Epistle to the Corinthians*, NICNT (Grand Rapids: Eerdmans, 1987), 433.

[4] Lewis Sperry Chafer, *Systematic Theology* (Grand Rapids: Kregel, 1993), 4:406.

14; cf. 4:13]), to be ready for the great day when he would see his Lord.

Precious indeed are his final words to his closest disciple, Timothy: "I have fought the good fight, I have finished the race, I have kept the faith. Finally, there is laid up for me the crown of righteousness, which the Lord, the righteous Judge, will give to me on that Day, and not to me only but also to all who have loved His appearing" (2 Tim. 4:7-8).

The apostle Peter had the same anticipation when he encouraged pastors to be "examples to the flock." Then he said, "When the Chief Shepherd appears, you will receive the crown of glory that does not fade away" (1 Peter 5:3-4).

The Apostle John warned his readers: "Look to yourselves, that we do not lose those things we worked for, but that we may receive a full reward" (2 John 8). And he recorded these solemn words from the Savior to the persecuted church at Smyrna: "Be faithful until death, and I will give you the crown of life" (Rev. 2:10). To the faithful church at Philadelphia (also in Asia), John recorded this challenge from Jesus: "Behold, I am coming quickly! Hold fast what you have, that no one may take your crown" (Rev. 3:11).

James, the half-brother of our Lord Jesus and pastor of the great "mother church" at Jerusalem, wrote: "Blessed is the man who endures temptation; for when he has been approved, he will receive the crown of life which the Lord has promised to those who love Him" (James 1:12).

But, someone might ask, "Why do I even need a reward or a crown? Isn't it enough to be assured of heaven with the Lord Jesus forever?" Even if most Christians would not actually say this, they often act as if the possibility of a reward provides no vital motivation for faithful Christian living and service.

The answer to such a question seems clear: the crown a believer might receive on that day will be for the Lord's honor, for we will "cast (our) crowns before the throne, saying: 'You are worthy, O Lord, to receive glory and honor'" (Rev. 4:10-11). Presumably, then, we will be ashamed if we have nothing to cast down before Him! Amazingly, even the Lord Jesus was motivated by the anticipation of a reward, for we are told that He, "for the joy that was set before Him endured the cross, despising the shame, and has sat down at the right hand of the throne of God" (Heb. 12:2).

As one writer has helpfully commented,

> I confess that I was surprised by the number of times Scripture uses rewards to motivate obedience. Like many of us, I tend toward the Kantian notion that we should simply do our duty for duty's sake and never think about reward. But that notion is quite unbiblical. If God takes the trouble (this many times!) to urge our obedience by a promise of reward, we should embrace that promise with thanks, not despise it. That is, we should not only do good works, but we should do them for this reason. This teaching, of course, is not salvation by works or merit. Although the word *reward* is used in these passages, there is no suggestion that we have earned the reward in the sense that we have paid God what the reward is worth. Jesus says that even when we have done everything commanded of us (and not one of us has done that), we have done no more than our duty (Luke 17:7-10). Indeed, in that case we are 'unworthy' servants. Elsewhere, Scripture represents the reward as something out of all proportion to the service rendered

(Matt. 19:29; 20:1-16; 25:45-46; 25:21-30; Luke 7:36-50; 12:37).[5]

The Judgment Seat in Paul, Peter, and John

The apostle Paul used the term *bema* when he wrote to the church at Corinth about our final confrontation with Christ to determine the gain or loss of rewards: "For we must all appear before the judgment seat [*bema*] of Christ, that each one may receive the things done in the body, according to what he has done, whether good or bad [*phaulon*, worthless]. Knowing, therefore, the terror of the Lord, we persuade men" (2 Cor. 5:10-11).

The Corinthians were very familiar with the word *bema*, for it was inscribed on the front of the large marble judgment throne where judicial issues were evaluated by the supreme judge, such as Gallio, the proconsul of Achaia, before whom Paul stood one day (cf. Acts 18:12, 16, 17). It was my privilege to see this *bema* during a trip to the ruins of ancient Corinth in August of 1952. Amazingly, it was before the *bema* of Pontius Pilate that our Lord took His stand (cf. Matt. 27:19; John 19:13).

To the church at Rome, Paul wrote, "We shall all stand before the judgment seat [*bema*] of Christ ... So then each of us shall give account of himself to God" (Rom. 14:10, 12). Even more ominous, perhaps, are the words of the apostle Peter: "For the time has come for judgment to begin at the house of God; and if it begins with us first, what will be the end of those who do not obey the gospel of God? Now 'If the

---

[5] John M. Frame, *The Doctrine of the Christian Life* (Phillipsburg, NJ: P&R, 2008), 283-84. See also Paul N. Benware, *The Believer's Payday* (Chattanooga: AMG, 2002).

righteous one is scarcely saved, where will the ungodly and the sinner appear?'" (1 Peter 4:17-18).

The apostle John warned his disciples ("little children"), "Abide in Him, that when He appears, we may have confidence and not be ashamed before Him at His coming" (1 John 2:28). D. Edmond Hiebert explains that the expression "be ashamed" describes "the feeling of personal shame of those who have fluctuated in their devotion and service and have allowed things to come into their lives which they will then recognize as evoking Christ's disapproval ... The picture is not of an unsaved individual but of a born-again believer who has allowed sin in his life because of slackness in his relationship with Christ. In support of this view is the first-person, plural subject of the verb ['we'], as denoting John and his readers."[6]

Christ's Qualifications for Judging Us

One fact that will be agreed upon by all Christians is that our Lord is fully equipped and qualified to examine and evaluate the thoughts, motives, words, and deeds of every member of His body, the Church. "Our God is a consuming fire" (Heb. 12:29), and He has "eyes like a flame of fire" (Rev. 1:14; cf. 19:12).

In fact, the Lord Jesus told us, "There is nothing covered that will not be revealed, nor hidden that will not be known. Therefore whatever you have spoken in the dark will be heard in the light, and what you have spoken in the ear in inner rooms will be proclaimed on the housetops" (Luke 12:2-3).

---

[6] D. Edmund Hiebert, *The Epistles of John* (Greenville, SC: Bob Jones University Press, 1991), 128.

The apostle Paul confirmed that "God will judge the secrets of men by Jesus Christ" (Rom. 2:16). These "secrets" include the motives behind all of our thoughts, words and actions. In other words, our God is infinitely concerned about the true reasons why we do and say things.

In this light, Paul could assure the Corinthian believers that it was not really so much what they thought of him that mattered. Infinitely more important was what God thought of him. "He who judges me is the Lord. Therefore judge nothing before the time, until the Lord comes, who will both bring to light the hidden things of darkness and reveal the counsels [motives] of the hearts. Then each one's praise will come from God" (1 Cor. 4:4-5).

When it comes to praise (or disapproval), it is what Christ says of us at the judgment seat that really counts.

The Impartiality of Christ's Judgment

Our Lord Jesus Christ will evaluate us some day, not only on the basis of our motives, but also on the basis of how much we knew of His will and Word, because "for everyone to whom much is given, from him much will be required" (Luke 12:48). Therefore, "that servant who knew his master's will, and did not prepare himself or do according to his will, shall be beaten with many stripes" (Luke 12:47).

But, if we did not know His will, are we not completely free of any consequences? No, for such ignorance is culpable: we should have done everything possible to learn His will for our lives through reading, believing, and obeying His Word! Here is an earthly illustration: What would happen to me if I were stopped by a traffic officer for driving 90 miles per hour though the city on my way to a conference? Would I be completely excused if I told him I didn't know what the speed limit was? His answer would be, "Sir, you are driving a dangerous machine! You should have found out what the speed limit is here. Explain your case to the judge!"

Mere human courts and judges, of course, cannot begin to compare with the absolute perfection of God's examination of people! That is because "the word of God is living and powerful, and sharper than any two-edged sword, piercing even to the division of soul and spirit, and of joints and marrow, and is a discerner of the thoughts and intents of the heart. And there is no creature hidden from His sight, but all things are naked and open to the eyes of Him to whom we must give account" (Heb. 4:12-13).

At the *bema* our Lord will show no partiality. "Whatever you do, do it heartily, as to the Lord and not to men, knowing that from the Lord you will receive the reward of the inheritance; for you serve the Lord Christ. But he [i.e., the Christian servant] who does wrong will be repaid for what he has done, and there is no partiality" (Col. 3:23-25). And Peter adds, "The Father ... without partiality judges according to each one's work" (1 Peter 1:17). Finally, the Bible ends with this word of divine assurance: "Behold, I am coming quickly, and My reward is with Me, to give to every one according to his work" (Rev. 22:12). To this, the apostle John, and hopefully each and every believer, responds: "Even so, come, Lord Jesus!" (Rev. 22:20).

The Most Detailed Description of the *Bema* of Christ

Paul had (under God) laid the foundation for the church at Corinth (cf. Acts 18:1-18), and Apollos of Alexandria, a disciple of John the Baptist (Acts 18:24-28), effectively built upon that foundation. But the Corinthians, in a fleshly way, polarized around one or the other of these faithful servants of God (1 Cor. 1:10-17).

Paul confronted this sectarian mentality as a basis for teaching the doctrine of the *bema*. "So then neither he who plants [i.e., Paul] is anything, nor he who waters [i.e., Apollos], but God who gives the increase. Now he who plants and he who waters are one, and each one will receive his own reward according to his own labor. For we are God's fellow workers; you are God's field, you are God's building. According to the grace of God which was given to me, as a wise master builder I have laid the foundation, and another builds on it. But let each one take heed how he builds on it [i.e., the foundation]. For no other foundation can anyone lay than that which is laid, which is Jesus Christ" (1 Cor. 3:7-11).

Thus, the discussion relates to the destiny of true, born-again believers only. What kind of superstructure has a Christian built upon his or her life in Christ? This is the supreme issue to be dealt with at the *bema* – for believers in ancient Corinth and for all of us today.

This is the heavy part of God's final word on this subject: "Now if anyone builds on this foundation (i.e., the finished work of Christ on the cross and His resurrection from the dead) with gold, silver, precious stones, wood, hay, straw, each one's work will become clear; for the Day will declare it, because it will be revealed by fire; and the fire will test each one's work, of what sort it is. If anyone's work which he has built on it endures, he will receive a reward. If anyone's work is burned, he will suffer loss; but he himself will be saved, yet so as through fire" (1 Cor. 3:12-15).

Tragically, hundreds of millions of people who claim to be Christians – namely, Roman Catholics – have been taught that this passage refers to purgatory, a place where imperfect Roman Catholics supposedly must pay for their sins, perhaps for centuries. (The horrible reality is that if we have to pay for our sins, we will never arrive in heaven.)

"But that is to miss Paul by a wide margin. This is metaphor, pure and simple. The Greek construction, *houtos de hos*, makes this certain: 'thus, as it were, only through fire.' [Paul is] probably reflecting something like Amos's 'firebrand plucked from the burning' (4:11)."[7]

Another author states: "The Roman Catholic interpretation completely misses the point. Paul is using an analogy. He is not talking about real fire. He is not talking about men and women burning. Paul is speaking of an imaginary building that represents a person's ministry, not the individual himself. Figuratively speaking, it is a person's work that will burn, not the person himself. The focus of the illustration is the potential loss of reward for poor service, not the atonement of sin or the cleansing of souls."[8]

Thus, everything we have said, done, and even thought as true Christians must be brought to full light. Could it be any other way? Can our Lord be deceived by mere outward religious forms and appearances? If any final recognition, honor, reward, or crown be granted to any of God's servants in that day, must it not be done in loving perfection? Will not all Christians, fully glorified and thus sinless on that great day,

---

[7] Fee, *The First Epistle to the Corinthians*, 144.

[8] James G. McCarthy, *The Gospel According to Rome* (Eugene, OR: Harvest House, 1995), 111. See also Mike Gendron, "The Fatal Fable of a Sin-Purifying Fire," *Proclaiming the Gospel* 18:2 (April-June, 2009, www.pro-gospel.org); Norman A. Olson, "Biblical Basis for Purgatory?" *Baptist Bulletin* (April, 2005), 9; and, especially, Norman Geisler, *Systematic Theology* (Minneapolis: Bethany House, 2005), 4:362-80. An official Roman Catholic statement may be found in *Catechism of the Catholic Church* (Liguori, MO: Liguori, 1944), 268-69.

agree totally with His final evaluation of each and every one of us?

Plainly, it is the unworthy works that will be burned, not the believers themselves! In fact, even though a believer's "work is burned ... he himself will be saved" (1 Cor. 3:15). But does that not reduce the *bema* confrontation to total insignificance? No, for "he will suffer loss ... as through fire" (v. 15). Does this mean, then, that some believers will be in a state of depression forever? "It would not be heaven if we were to spend eternity in sadness because of what we did not do. Undoubtedly there will be regret, but our overwhelming emotion will be the realization of the wonderful grace of God that saved us and brought us to heaven. There will be rejoicing in heaven instead of tears."[9]

The Long-term Effects of the *Bema*

No matter what loss of reward a Christian may experience at the judgment seat of Christ, he or she will be eternally grateful to be there. Only born-again Christians are allowed to see Him on that awesome occasion. As the apostle John expressed it, "Beloved, now we are children of God; and it has not yet been revealed what we shall be, but we know that when He is revealed, we shall be like Him, for we shall see Him as He is. And everyone who has this hope in Him purifies himself, just as He is pure" (1 John 3:2-3).

Each of us, as members of His body, will be in total agreement with His evaluation of us. There will be no complaining and no appeal to a higher court. In fact, we will humbly participate in the divine process of preparing us for the marriage of the Lamb, which occurs in heaven seven years after

---

[9] John Walvoord, "Believer's Day of Reward," in *Understanding Christian Theology*, ed. Charles Swindoll & Roy Zuck (Nashville: Nelson, 2003), 1279.

the rapture of the Church and just before our Lord's glorious second coming. At that time, we are told, "'Let us be glad and rejoice and give Him glory, for the marriage of the Lamb has come, and His wife has made herself ready.' And to her it was granted to be arrayed in fine linen, clean and bright, for the fine linen is the righteous acts of the saints" (Rev. 19:7-8).

No, the body and bride of Christ will not be split apart, with some reigning with Him and other believers excluded from this privilege. Our Lord made this promise to His disciples in the Upper Room: "I will come again and receive you to Myself; that where I am, there you may be also" (John 14:3). And the apostle John tells us, "Blessed and holy is he who has part in the first resurrection. Over such the second death has no power, but they shall be priests of God and of Christ, and shall reign with Him a thousand years" (Rev. 20:6).

Does this include believers who have brought great disappointment to our Lord? Yes, for among the most carnal-minded Christians Paul ever had to deal with were those in the church at Corinth. And to them he wrote, "Do you not know that the saints will judge the world? And if the world will be judged by you, are you unworthy to judge the smallest matters? Do you not know that we shall judge angels? How much more, things that pertain to this life?" (1 Cor. 6:2-3).

God graciously gives to every person wonderful opportunities and responsibilities, especially toward Himself, our Creator and Lord. Some will accept these and build upon them. Others will reject them. That is one of the lessons of His parable of the talents (Matt. 25:14-30). To one person the master gave five talents – a fabulous amount, financially speaking. To another he gave two talents, and to another one talent, to invest "each according to his own ability" (v. 15).

The first two immediately invested their talents to have something to give to their master upon his return from a long journey. But the third man despised his gift and put it into a hole in the ground. When the master finally returned, the first two showed deep respect for him and were rewarded. The third man said to him, "Lord, I knew you to be a hard man, reaping where you have not sown, and gathering where you have not scattered seed. And I was afraid, and went and hid your talent in the ground. Look, there you have what is yours" (Matt. 25:24-25).

D. A. Carson observes that this servant "is saying that the master is grasping, exploiting the labor of others ... and putting the servant in an invidious position ... (and thus) betrays his lack of love for his master, which he masks by blaming his master and excusing himself."[10]

Obviously, the first two men in the parable represent believers, who use their God-given gifts for His glory. The third man represents unbelievers. No true believer will experience the destiny of this man, of whom the master says, "Cast the unprofitable servant into the outer darkness. There will be weeping and gnashing of teeth" (Matt. 25:30).

Our Lord makes no mistakes in judgment. He is infinitely gracious, loving, and generous. But He also requires accountability. That is a basic part of our possession of His image and likeness.[11]

Forgiveness Now – But Fire Later?

At the judgment seat of Christ, it will be unworthy works that will be burned, not the believers! Thank God! Even though a believer's "work is burned ... he himself will be

---

[10] D. A. Carson, "Matthew," in *The Expositor's Bible Commentary*, ed. Frank E. Gaebelein (Grand Rapids: Zondervan, 1984), 8:517.

[11] Excellent papers on the destiny of believers at the *bema* are available from George Zeller at www.MiddletownBibleChurch.org.

saved" (1 Cor. 3:15). "He will suffer loss ... as through fire," yet as noted earlier, "there will be rejoicing in heaven instead of tears."[12]

How, then, do we relate all of this to the forgiveness and cleansing He provides for us when we confess our sins, for "if we confess our sins, He is faithful and just to forgive us our sins and to cleanse us from all unrighteousness" (1 John 1:9)? If we confess our sins now, does this cancel out any potential loss of rewards at the *bema*?

David and Bathsheba

Perhaps the clearest answer to this question is provided for us in 2 Samuel 12. King David had sinned grievously against the Lord by having one of his faithful generals, Uriah the Hittite, killed in order to obtain his wife Bathsheba (see 2 Sam. 11). When David refused to confess his sin, God sent Nathan the prophet to him. Nathan related a tragic story about a rich man who took a poor man's "one little ewe lamb" to prepare it for a guest (2 Sam. 12:3).

David, of course, was enraged: "As the LORD lives, the man who has done this shall surely die!" (2 Sam. 12:5).

"Then Nathan said to David, 'You are the man! ... Now therefore, the sword shall never depart from your house, because you have despised Me, and have taken the wife of Uriah the Hittite to be your wife'" (2 Sam. 12:7, 10).

That did it. David immediately saw the magnitude of his own sin and cried out, "I have sinned against the LORD" (2 Sam. 12:13). Psalm 51 is a profound expression of David's deep and genuine repentance to God: "I acknowledge my transgressions, and my sin is always before me. Against You, You only, have I sinned, and done this evil in Your sight – that

---

[12] Walvoord, "Believer's Day of Reward," 1279.

You may be found just when You speak, and blameless when You judge" (Ps. 51:3-4).

Now did this genuine confession change anything? Yes! Nathan replied immediately, "The LORD also has put away your sin; you shall not die" (2 Sam. 12:13). Then was everything wonderful again? No! Nathan went on to say, "However, because by this deed you have given great occasion to the enemies of the LORD to blaspheme, the child also who is born to you shall surely die" (v. 14). Furthermore, he said, "The sword shall never depart from your house ... I will raise up adversity against you from your own house" (vv. 10-11). Among the disasters that followed were the horrible sins and rebellions of his sons Absalom, Amnon, and Adonijah.

Did the LORD truly forgive David? Yes!

Were the full consequences of his sin totally wiped out? No!

That is the ultimate issue. When we truly confess our sins, God graciously forgives us and restores fellowship with us. But the full consequences of our sins must still be brought to light and dealt with by the LORD. That will be the function and purpose of the *bema*.

The Public Testimony of Believers

What concerns our loving Lord is not only His daily relationship with each of His children but also the long-term impact and influence of our Christian lives and ministries upon others. This is especially true with regard to Christian leaders. For example, if the pastor of a church commits a serious public sin, his position of leadership in the church is (with possible rare exceptions) finished, even though he might genuinely confess his sin to God.

As Paul wrote to Timothy, "A bishop then must be blameless ... he must have a good testimony among those who are outside, lest he fall into reproach and the snare of the devil" (1 Tim. 3:2, 7). And, "Be an example to the believers in word, in conduct, in love, in spirit, in faith, in purity" (1 Tim. 4:12).

To the great church at Ephesus, Paul wrote, "But fornication and all uncleanness or covetousness, let it not even be named among you, as is fitting for saints" (Eph. 5:3). And to Titus, a church planter on the island of Crete, he wrote, "Appoint elders in every city as I commanded you – if a man is blameless, the husband of one wife" (Titus 1:5-6).

In his final chapter, the author of Hebrews concluded: "Marriage is honorable among all, and the bed undefiled; but fornicators and adulterers God will judge" (Heb. 13:4). James, the half-brother of Jesus and pastor of the "mother church" in Jerusalem, warned, "My brethren, let not many of you become teachers, knowing that we shall receive a stricter judgment" (James 3:1).

The public doesn't know and certainly does not even care about whether such a church leader has made a personal confession to God. What the public does care about – and will probably never forget – is his public sin. This deeply hurts and grieves our Lord and will surely be a major factor in determining the gain or loss of a reward or crown at the *bema*. "Do not grieve the Holy Spirit of God, by whom you were sealed for the day of redemption" (Eph. 4:30).

"Adultery is not the only sin that disqualifies a minister from office, but it is one of the more visible and confusing sins plaguing the church of our time. What is particularly troublesome about this sin is the abuse of (pastoral authority) that often attends it. Deep pain is brought to the sexual partner in a clergy affair, and even deeper pain to the minister's wife. The minister, given an honored office through which he is called to serve abused and vulnerable people, violates that very trust by becoming, himself, a violator ... Many borrow psychotherapeutic concepts such as healing and recovery as rationales for returning to pastoral ministry, but with no genuine recognition of the pathology that manifests itself in the abuse of (pastoral authority)."[13]

Thus, God intends the bema confrontation to motivate each and every believer – not just church leaders – to serve Him "in spirit and truth" (John 4:24). It has not been designed by our Savior to be a horrible threat that produces fear and depression but rather an encouragement to love Him and to obey and serve Him from the heart.

In this light, may we, as Christians, be more concerned than ever before about our testimony for the Head of the Church, the Bridegroom of the Bride, who loves us with infinite love, and who paid the ultimate price for our redemption and future glorification.

---

[13] R. Kent Hughes and John H. Armstrong, "Why Adulterous Pastors Should Not Be Restored: Repentance Is Not Enough for Restoring Fallen Ministers to the Pulpit," *Christianity Today* (April 3, 1995), 34.

3

The Church Is Not Israel!

Many Christian scholars insist that God is finished with Israel and that the promises He made to that nation have been transferred to the Church. However, it is crucial to a correct understanding of God's plan for the ages that the Church not be confused with Israel. The Bible itself makes the distinction between the Church and Israel clear and leads us to four important conclusions.

True Worship During the Great Tribulation Will Be Distinctively Israelite Rather Than Distinctively Christian

Our Lord Jesus Christ warned Israelite believers to pray that during the Great Tribulation that their "flight will not be … on a Sabbath" (Matt. 24:20). Only Israel, not the Church, is under a divinely enforced Sabbath law. The apostle Paul warned the Church, "No one is to act as your judge in regard to … a Sabbath day" (Col. 2:16; cf. Rom. 14:5). In ancient Israel, the death penalty was even inflicted on one who prepared a meal on the Sabbath (Num. 15:32-36; cf. Exod. 35:2-3). Thus, no one today, not even the Seventh-day Adventist, is truly observing the Sabbath.

Our Lord Jesus Christ also warned Israelite believers that the Abomination of Desolation would stand "in the holy place" (Matt. 24:15). Only Israel, not the Church, can have a legitmate "holy place" on this earth. Our Lord stated to the Samaritan woman, "An hour is coming when neither in this mountain, nor in Jerusalem, will you worship the Father" (John 4:21). However, Paul spoke of the future "man of lawlessness" who "takes his seat in the temple of God" (2 Thess. 2:3-4; cf. Rev. 11:1-2).

During the coming Tribulation, there will be an altar in the temple for the offering of divinely approved animal sacrifices.[1] However, the Church has no altar on earth, nor are animals to be sacrificed (1 Cor. 11:23-26; Heb. 10:1-14; 13:15; 1 Peter 2:5; Rom. 15:16). The temple and the altar for sacrifice will be divinely ordained in Jerusalem during this future period and will not be a mere Jewish cultural center. However, the outer court will be given over to the Gentile nations to desecrate during the last half of the Seventieth Week of Daniel (Rev. 11:2).

The only way the Antichrist will be able to break his seven-year covenant with Israel and to cause the blood sacrifices and the grain offerings to cease (Dan. 9:27) will be to kill God's two witnesses in Jerusalem (Rev. 11:7-12). It is difficult to see

---

[1] See the discussion below, as well as chapters 11 and 12. See also Renald E. Showers, *There Really Is a Difference* (Bellmawr, NJ: Friends of Israel, 1990); W. R. Willis and J. R. Master, eds., *Issues in Dispensationalism* (Chicago: Moody, 1994); Tim LaHaye and Ed Hindson, *The Popular Prophecy Workbook* (Eugene: Harvest House, 2006); John F. Walvoord, *The Church in Prophecy*, rev. ed. (Grand Rapids: Kregel, 1999); Charles C. Ryrie, *Revelation*, new ed. (Chicago: Moody, 1996); Charles C. Ryrie, ed., *Countdown to Armageddon* (Eugene: Harvest House, 1999); Michael J. Vlach, *Dispensationalism* (Los Angeles: Theological Studies Press, 2008); Thomas Ice and Timothy Demy, eds., *The Return* (Grand Rapids: Kregel, 1999); Paul N. Benware, *Understanding End Times Prophecy: A Comprehensive Approach*, new ed. (Chicago: Moody, 2006); John F. Walvoord, *The Prophecy Knowledge Handbook* (Wheaton: Victor, 1990).

how blood sacrifices could be offered on the Jerusalem altar during those first three and a half years if the two witnesses of God did not approve of this form of worship; for their teaching ministry will be supernaturally enforced (Rev. 11:3-6), even to the destruction of all enemies. Thus, they will authoritatively set the pattern for the true worship of God on earth following the rapture of the Church.

Not only will there be a God-approved temple and altar with appropriate sacrifices in Tribulation Jerusalem, but there will also be, of necessity, Levitical priests to carry out this Israelite form of worship. Ever since Roman armies destroyed the temple and its genealogical records in AD 70, Jews have been unable to determine their precise tribal identity. Thus, there can be no legitimate Israelite worship during the Church age.

However, during the early part of Daniel's Seventieth Week, God will reveal the true tribal identity of at least 144,000 Israelites (Rev. 7:4-8), and among these will be 12,000 Levites (v. 7). It seems probable that this will be revealed through the two witnesses, for Zerubbabel asserted that lost priestly records could not be recovered "until a priest stood up with Urim and Thummim" (Ezra 2:63). This has yet to happen and cannot happen until the bride of Christ has been removed from the earth by rapture. It also will probably be through the testimony of the two witnesses that the 12,000 Levites (among others) will be won to a saving knowledge of the God of Israel. This assumption is based on the biblical principle that conversion can come only through men who are sent by God (Rom. 10:14-15). With the Church now in heaven (cf. Rev. 3:10), the only witnesses on earth just after the rapture will be these two men. It will be through their supernaturally confirmed and protected instructions, therefore, that converted Levites will understand how to offer legitimate sacrifices at the Jerusalem altar. God describes them as "the two olive trees and the two lampstands that stand before the Lord of the earth" (Rev. 11:4). In similar fashion, it was through the ministry of two Old Testament "olive trees," or "anointed ones" (i.e., Joshua the high priest and Zerubbabel the governor, Zech. 4:3, 14), that the new altar in Jerusalem and its sacrifices were established following the Babylonian captivity, even before the temple was rebuilt (Ezra 3:1-6).[2]

A foundational truth of Christian ecclesiology is the unity of the body of Christ. Thus, it is unthinkable that the true Church could ever have a distinct Jewish subdivision. The apostle Paul insisted that Christ "broke down the barrier of the dividing wall" (Eph. 2:14) so that now "there is no distinction between Greek and Jew" (Col. 3:11), and we are thus "all one in Christ Jesus" (Gal. 3:28).

Therefore, it is biblically impossible to have the bride of Christ bearing witness to her Lord throughout the Seventieth Week of Daniel with one segment of the bride doing distinctively Christian things and another segment, divided into twelve tribes, doing distinctively Jewish things! The angel Gabriel made it clear to Daniel, after all, that "the seventy weeks [including the seventieth!] have been decreed for your people and your holy city" (Dan. 9:24).

True Worship on the Earth During the Coming Kingdom Age Will Be Distinctively Israelite Rather Than Distinctively Christian

The Bible provides abundant testimony to the Israelite form of worship that will characterize the kingdom age. The temple, which will be the focus of worship on the earth during

---

[2] For further discussion of this issue, see chapter 7 under the heading "The Time of Their Ministry."

the thousand-year reign of Christ, is described in much detail by Joel (3:18), Isaiah (2:2), Daniel (9:24), Ezekiel (40–48), and Haggai (2:7, 9).

Furthermore, the animal sacrifices that will be offered in that temple are carefully described in Isaiah (56:6-7; 60:7), Jeremiah (33:18), Zechariah (14:16-21), and especially in Ezekiel (40–46).

God even stated, through Jeremiah, that just as "David shall never lack a man to sit on the throne of the house of Israel," so "the Levitical priests shall never lack a man before Me to offer burnt offerings, to burn grain offerings, and to prepare sacrifices continually" (Jer. 33:17-18).[3] Ezekiel goes even further and narrows down these Levitical priests to the family of Zadok, who was faithful to King David to the very end (Ezek. 40:46; 43:19; 44:15; 48:11; cf. 1 Kings 1:34).

Inevitably, those who deny that true worship on earth during the Great Tribulation will be distinctively Israelite also go on to deny that true worship during the Millennium will be distinctively Israelite.[4]

Serious Theological Error Results from Every Effort to Incorporate Israelite Functions into the Church

- By denying to Israel her functional distinctives, Christians fall under the warning of the apostle Paul: "Do not be arrogant toward the [Israelite] branches ... so that you will not be wise in your own estimation" (Rom. 11:18, 25).

---

[3] See chapter 11, especially point 5 under "Arguments in Support of a Literal Interpretation.

[4] For a defense of a literal interpretation of God's covenants with Israel, see Alva J. McClain, *The Greatness of the Kingdom* (Winona Lake, IN: BMH Books, 1959).

- The hermeneutical error and danger of denying the clear revelation of God's prophetic program for Israel also results: "O foolish men and slow of heart to believe in all that the prophets have spoken!" (Luke 24:25).
- The soteriological error of mixing Mosaic and Christian programs and thus falling into the heresy of Galatianism (Gal. 3:1-3) is a tragic consequence of the confusion of the Church and Israel.
- Confusing Israel's distinct pattern of government, society, and economics with the Great Commission of our Lord Jesus Christ to His Church is another result.

This mentality was a very influential factor in the formation of the Roman Catholic Church. Note also the trends in Seventh-day Adventism and other socioeconomic cults. Finally, watch carefully the rise of postmillennialism within evangelical Protestantism and the "two-pronged gospel," or social/political/evangelism blend that characterizes the neo-evangelical movement today.[5]

Similarities Between Israel and the Church Cannot Be Used to Obscure Their Profound Differences

Similarities

Israel and the Church do share some basic similarities.
- They worship the same God.
- They are related to this living and sovereign God through the same basic plan of salvation (divine election and justification by grace through the merits of

---

[5] For a critique of the "two-pronged Gospel," see Gary T. Meadors, "John R. W. Stott on Social Action," *Grace Theological Journal* 1:2 (Fall, 1980), 129-147.

Christ's blood and through faith in His Word; and regeneration and indwelling by the Holy Spirit with the same hope of future glorification).

- They share the same divinely normative moral standards.

Differences

The differences between Israel and the Church are equally important to recognize.

- The Church, as the bride of Christ, was first established on the Day of Pentecost by means of the Son of God baptizing people in the Holy Spirit into His body (Acts 1:5; 11:15-18).
- The Church has been given a unique commission and message, as well as freedom from the nonnormative aspects of the Law of Moses (including the Sabbath and other holy days, a special group of priests, and a geographically localized holy land and city and altar for animal sacrifices).

Since these similarities and differences are clearly explained to us by God in such passages as Romans 11 and Ephesians 2–3, it is vitally important for us, as God's people today, to build our Christian lives and ministries solidly upon the rock of biblical revelation. No other foundation can withstand the inevitable pressures that a sinful and satanic world system will bring.

"Pay close attention to yourself and to your teaching; persevere in these things; for as you do this you will ensure salvation both for yourself and for those who hear you" (1 Tim. 4:16).

4

Could Christ Return This Year?

The biblical answer to this burning question is – yes and no! *Yes*, He could return from heaven at any moment now to meet His true Church – His body and bride – in the air. And, therefore, *no* – He will not come down to the earth during the next twelve months. His return to the earth will occur seven years after the Church has been caught up to heaven.

Why does the Bible make this distinction? Because the *second coming of our Lord*, just like His *first coming*, is a complex series of events covering a number of years. Think for a moment of the *first coming*. It began with the miraculous conception of the God-man in the womb of a Jewish woman about 4 BC. Then came His birth, growth, public ministry, death, burial, resurrection, and ascension back to heaven – requiring more than a third of a century.

So also, the *second coming of Christ* will cover a number of years, beginning with the resurrection of dead Christians and the rapture of living Christians (1 Thess. 4:13-18). Then, for the Church, there will be a period of examination by her Bridegroom to determine gain or loss of rewards (1 Cor. 3:10-15), culminating in "the marriage of the Lamb" (Rev. 19:7-9).

In the meantime, on the earth, a number of spectacular things will take place, requiring eighty-four months, or seven years (Rev. 11:2-3), before He sets foot again on this planet (Zech. 14:4). Two witnesses will suddenly appear in Jerusalem, one of whom will be Elijah (Mal. 4:5-6, Rev. 11:3-6). After they have led the nation of Israel back to God (Matt. 17:11), they will be killed by the Antichrist (Rev. 11:7-13). But during the last three and a half years of the Tribulation period, 144,000 of their disciples, from the twelve tribes of Israel, will take "this gospel of the kingdom . . . to all the nations" (Matt. 24:14; cf. Rev. 7:3-8; 14:1-5).

As soon as the Church is removed from the earth (John 14:1-3; 2 Thess. 2:1-8), the "little horn" (i.e., "the Antichrist," or "the Beast") will be launched by Christ Himself into his steady march to global dominion (Dan. 7:8; Rev. 6:1-2). He will make a firm covenant with the majority of Israelis for a seven-year period (Dan. 9:27) and lead them to international prestige.

After forty-two months, the Antichrist is killed (presumably by the King of the North; Dan. 11:40-45; Rev. 13:14), but he rises again to mortal life and kills his archenemies, the two witnesses (Rev. 11:7-13). He then turns against Israel (which is by now a basically converted nation; Isa. 66:8; Rev. 12:1-6, 13-16), stops the temple sacrifices (Dan. 9:27), sets up "the abomination of desolation" in the temple of God (Matt. 24:15, KJV), and demands worship of himself with horrible consequences for those who refuse to submit (Rev. 13:11-17). Under Satan's direction, he will gather the armies of the world to challenge the Lord Jesus Christ at His glorious second coming to the earth (Ps. 2:1-6; Rev. 16:12-16; 19:19).

By means of these complex events, God will prepare the Church, the nation of Israel, and the Gentile nations for His glorious one-thousand-year kingdom on earth.

But when will all of this begin to happen? We wish we knew – but our Lord warned us about setting the date! "But of that day or hour no one knows, not the angels in heaven, nor the Son, but the Father alone" (Mark 13:32). Now think of this statement! Our Lord knew that the exact date was unknown to all mere humans, and to all of heaven's angels, and even to Himself (during the nonglorified phase of His incarnation)! The Lord Jesus had set aside the independent exercise of certain attributes of greatness (such as omniscience) at His first coming (Phil. 2:5-8; Luke 2:52). But He remained totally divine and totally sinless, and He received from His Father a perfect understanding of the temporary limits of His knowledge (John 5:20).

This year could see the beginning of Second Coming events! For believers today, this is the blessed hope, for we know that "when He appears, we will be like Him, because we will see Him just as He is" (1 John 3:2). But for all mankind, our Lord gave this urgent warning: "Take heed, keep on the alert; for you do not know when the appointed time will come. ... What I say to you I say to all, 'Be on the alert!'" (Mark 13:33, 37).

To which we should joyfully reply, "Amen. Come, Lord Jesus" (Rev. 22:20).

PART 2

THE TRIBULATION AND CHRIST'S RETURN

5

Daniel's Great Seventy-Weeks Prophecy

It has often been said, and I believe with truth, that those who shun the study of biblical languages will find themselves at the mercy of the translators. Nowhere is this more true than in the case of the Hebrew Old Testament, as may be seen by the discussions that have been provoked by recent translations of the Old Testament.

One purpose of this study is to encourage an interest in the study of Hebrew exegesis for the purpose of determining the exact meaning of the Old Testament text. Another purpose is to show how the study of one Hebrew word can help to unlock the mysteries of one of the most fascinating prophecies of the entire Old Testament: the seventy-weeks prophecy of Daniel.

The first great problem that confronts us as we seek the interpretation of this prophecy is the meaning of the Hebrew word *shābûa'*, which is translated in our English versions by the word *week*. We must now examine the entire prophecy as found in Daniel 9:24-27, and as translated in the New American Standard Bible, calling special attention to the word *week*, which appears six times within the four verses.

Seventy weeks have been decreed for your people and your holy city, to finish the transgression, to make an end of sin, to make atonement for iniquity, to bring in everlasting righteousness, to seal up vision and prophecy and to anoint the most holy place. So you are to know and discern that from the issuing of a decree to restore and rebuild Jerusalem until Messiah the Prince there will be seven weeks and sixty-two weeks; it will be built again, with plaza and moat, even in times of distress. Then after the sixty-two weeks the Messiah will be cut off and have nothing, and the people of the prince who is to come will destroy the city and the sanctuary. And its end will come with a flood; even to the end there will be war; desolations are determined. And he will make a firm covenant with the many for one week, but in the middle of the week he will put a stop to sacrifice and grain offering; and on the wing of abominations will come one who makes desolate, even until a complete destruction, one that is decreed, is poured out on the one who makes desolate.

Our problem is to determine how long a period of time is intended by this word: whether a week of *days,* as the most common usage of the word would suggest, or whether, perhaps, it is intended to be a week of *years,* as the immediate context would seem to demand. The problem is intensified by the fact that nowhere else in the Old Testament, when the word is used by itself, does it mean anything else than a week of *days*.[1]

In seeking a solution to this interesting and important problem, we shall study the word *shābûa'* ("week") in the light of analogous Hebrew usage, comparative chronology, and the context of biblical prophecy.

Hebrew Usage

The dictionary definition of our English word *week* is "a period of seven successive days."[2] This is not true of the Hebrew *shābûa'*. Its literal meaning is "a unit of seven."[3] It has no primary reference to time periods at all, whether of days or years. In other words, it is simply a numerical measure. Let us demonstrate what we mean by examining a similar Hebrew word. The word *'āsôr* would seem to have the basic meaning of "ten days," because that is its correct translation in thirteen out of the sixteen times it appears in the Old Testament.[4] But

---

[1] The noun *shābûa'* appears 20 times in 17 verses: Gen. 29:27, 28; Exod. 34:22; Lev. 12:5; Num. 28:26; Deut. 16:9 (2x), 10, 16; 2 Chron. 8:13; Jer. 5:24; Ezek. 45:21; Dan. 9:24, 25 (2x), 26, 27 (2x), 10:2, 3. See Gerhard Lisowsky, *Konkordanz zum Hebraischen Alten Testament* (Stuttgart: Württembergische Bibelanstalt, 1958), 1395-96.

[2] C. L. Barnhart, ed., *The American College Dictionary* (New York: Random House, 1964), s.v. "week."

[3] See Francis Brown, S. R. Driver, and Charles A. Briggs, *A Hebrew and English Lexicon of the Old Testament* (Oxford: Clarendon, 1978), 988-89; William L. Holladay, *A Concise Hebrew and Aramaic Lexicon of the Old Testament* (Grand Rapids: Eerdmans, 1971), 358; L. Koehler and W. Baumgartner, eds., *Hebräisches und Aramäisches Lexikon* (Leiden: Brill, 1967), 940.

[4] The noun *'āsôr* refers to days in Gen. 24:55; Exod. 12:3; Lev. 6:29; 23:27; 25:9; Num. 29:7; Josh. 4:19; 2 Kings. 25:1; Jer. 52:4, 12; Ezek. 20:1; 24:1; 40:1. See Lisowsky, *Konkordanz*, 1137.

on three occasions it does not mean "ten days" at all but rather "ten strings," or "an instrument of ten strings": Psalm 33:2; 92:3 (92:4, Heb.); 144:9.[5] Therefore the word *'āsôr* must mean "decad," or "unit of ten," and whether it means "ten days" or "ten strings" must be determined entirely by the context, not by the word itself.[6]

On the basis of analogous Hebrew usage, therefore, we find that our word *shābûa'* may have the basic meaning of "heptad," or "unit of seven," even as *'āsôr* must mean "decad," or "unit of ten." This possibility is greatly strengthened by the fact that *shābûa'* appears three times in the Old Testament with the word *yāmîm* ("days") added, as though to imply that *shābûa'* by itself was not sufficient to show that a period of seven days was intended.[7] The most interesting point, however, is that two of these three combinations of *shābûa'* and *yāmîm* appear in the second and third verses of Daniel 10,[8] immediately following the seventy weeks prophecy of the preceding chapter, as though to warn the reader that *shābûa'* is now being used in a different sense!

Comparative Chronology

If the seventy-weeks prophecy refers to weeks (sevens) of years, we are then dealing with a time span of seventy sevens of years, or 490 years. Now according to the second verse of this same ninth chapter of Daniel, the prophet Daniel had

---

[5] Ibid.

[6] See Brown, Driver, and Briggs, *A Hebrew and English Lexicon*, 797; Holladay, *Lexicon*, 285; Koehler and Baumgartner, *Hebräisches und Aramäisches Lexikon*, 741.

[7] The terms *shābûa'* and *yôm* occur together in Ezek. 45:21; Dan. 10:2; and Dan. 10:3. See Lisowsky, *Konkordanz*, 1195.

[8] Ibid.

been studying the prophecy of Jeremiah 25:11-12, which stated that Israel's captivity in Babylon would last for exactly seventy years. It was because this seventy-year period had now come to an end that Daniel began to pray for the deliverance of his people Israel, in accordance with Jeremiah's prophecy.

The full significance of the seventy-year captivity in Babylon does not come to light, however, until we consider some explanatory passages in Leviticus and 2 Chronicles. Leviticus 25:2-5 states that every seventh year the children of Israel were to observe "a sabbath rest" for the land, during which time they were to neither sow their fields nor prune their vineyards for an entire year. Then in chapter 26, verses 34, 35, and 43, a solemn warning was added, that if this commandment was not obeyed, the people would be sent into captivity, and the land would be left desolate for a number of years equal to the number of sabbath-rest years that they failed to observe.

Now when we turn to the account of Jerusalem's destruction by Nebuchadnezzar in 2 Chronicles 36, we read in verse 21 that the purpose of the captivity was "to fulfill the word of the Lord by the mouth of Jeremiah, until the land had enjoyed its sabbaths. All the days of its desolation it kept sabbath until seventy years were complete." On the basis of these passages, therefore, we may conclude that the seventy-year captivity of Israel in Babylon came about as a result of a lax attitude toward the Law of Moses, as evidenced by her failure to observe a total of seventy different Levitical sabbath-rest years, over a period of 490 years.

These facts lead us to make the following observations: If 490 years of disobedience had brought 70 years of punishment, is it not *probable* that the testing period for Israel which was now announced to Daniel would cover another 490 *years*, instead of 490 *days*? How could all the events described in this prophecy have taken place within a period of less than seventeen months (490 days)? And what comfort would it have brought to Daniel and his people to be told that only a year and a half after the termination of the Babylonian captivity, their city would be destroyed again? And, finally, where in the history of this period can a destruction of the city and sanctuary be seen? Comparative chronology, therefore, makes it *probable* that sevens of *years*, rather than sevens of *days*, is to be understood by the word *shābûa'* in this prophecy.

The Context of Biblical Prophecy

Turning first to Daniel 7:25, we read of the coming of a wicked person who "will speak out against the Most High ... and he will intend to make alterations in times and in law; and they will be given into his hand for a time, times, and half a time." Our purpose here is not to discuss the identity of this person but to determine the meaning of the phrase, "a time, times, and half a time," which appears not only here, but also in Daniel 12:7 and Revelation 12:14.

It is in Revelation 12 that we discover the clear interpretation of that phrase. The fourteenth verse reads as follows: "The two wings of the great eagle were given to the woman, so that she could fly into the wilderness to her place, where she was nourished for a time and times and half a time." Comparing this with verse 6, we read: "Then the woman fled into the wilderness where she had a place prepared by God, so that there she would be nourished for one thousand two hundred and sixty days." This same period of tribulation is mentioned also in Revelation 11:3 as being 1,260 days in length, while in 11:2 and 13:5 it is given as 42 months. It is, of course, a matter of simple arithmetic to demonstrate that 1,260 days is equivalent to 42 thirty-day months, or approximately three and a half *years*, or, in other words, "a year and two years and half a year."

It goes without saying that this particular time period, which is mentioned in seven different texts, in three different ways, and in two different books, must play a tremendously important part in biblical prophecy. With this in mind, let us turn once again to Daniel's seventy-weeks prophecy. The last part of Daniel 9:26 speaks of a person who will bring great destruction to the land and people of Israel, especially with regard to Jerusalem and its temple. Carrying this thought a bit further, the prophecy goes on to explain in verse 27 that "he will make a firm covenant with the many for one week, but in the middle of the week he will put a stop to sacrifice and grain offering ... even until a complete destruction, one that is decreed, is poured out on the one who makes desolate."

The laws of biblical interpretation demand that single verses or passages of prophecy be interpreted in the light of their immediate context, and ultimately in the light of the entire context of biblical prophecy. Applying this tried and proven principle to the passage under consideration, is it not evident that the destructive person mentioned here is the same as the one in Daniel 7 and also in Revelation? And is it not likewise evident that we have the same period of tribulation here as in the other passages, which we have shown elsewhere to be three and a half years in length? If the probability of these assumptions be admitted, then we are led to the conclusion that the word *shābûa'* in Daniel's seventy-weeks prophecy means a period of seven *years*, not seven days.

Daniel 9:27 represents this destructive person as making a covenant with many people that lasts for seven time-units. Then, in the midst of this period, which would correspond to the three-and-a-half time-unit mark, he breaks the covenant and brings about a period of tribulation that lasts for the

remaining three-and-a-half time-units until "a complete destruction, one that is decreed, is poured out on the one who
makes desolate." Since the time period of tribulation in the
other passages is definitely three and half *years* in length, does
it not seem reasonable to suppose that the three and a half
time-units of tribulation in Daniel's prophecy are likewise
years?

These three different converging lines of reasoning have
finally brought us to the place where we can say with confidence that while the word *shābûa'*, meaning "unit of seven,"
has reference to *days* in most of its Old Testament occurrences
because of the demands of context, it has reference to *years* in
the ninth chapter of Daniel, likewise because of the demands
of context. A careful study of this interesting Hebrew word
has thus laid for us a solid foundation upon which we may
build our further study of one of the most fascinating prophecies in the entire Bible.[9]

---

[9] See Paul D. Feinberg, "An Exegetical and Theological Study of Daniel
9:24-27," in *Tradition and Testament,* ed. John and Paul Feinberg (Chicago:
Moody, 1981), 189-200; Christopher Cone, ed., *Dispensationalism Tomorrow
and Beyond* (Ft. Worth: Tyndale Seminary Press, 2008); and John Mac-
Arthur and Richard Mayhue, eds., *Christ's Prophetic Plans* (Chicago:
Moody, 2012).

6

Daniel and the Antichrist

What will the world be like just before the second coming of Christ? Our Lord emphasized the enormous potential of global deception at that time. In answer to the disciples' urgent question, "What will be the sign of Your coming, and of the end of the age?" (Matt. 24:3), our Lord warned them: "See to it that no one misleads you. For many will come in My name ... and will mislead many ... Many false prophets will arise and will mislead many. ... For false Christs and false prophets will arise and will show great signs and wonders, so as to mislead, if possible, even the elect" (Matt. 24:4-5, 11, 24). Note the emphasis on the words *false* and *mislead* in our Lord's answer!

One moment after the rapture of the Church, every surviving religious leader in the world will be a false one! Yes, millions of good gospel tracts, books, and taped messages will still be here, but all born-again Christians will be gone. Human reflectors of the Light of the World will be in heaven with their Savior. Suddenly, the worst person the world has even seen will introduce himself to the people of Israel and will offer to them hope for security and military victory in the midst of a world that hates them – this is the Antichrist! He is the one of whom the Lord Jesus said, "I have come in My Father's name, and you did not receive Me; if another shall come in his own name, you will receive him" (John 5:43).

So the true Christ knows about the future Antichrist? Of course! In fact, our Lord will actually launch him into his seven-year career on planet earth: "I saw when the Lamb [Jesus] broke one of the seven seals, and I heard one of the four living creatures saying as with a voice of thunder, 'Come.' And I looked, and behold, a white horse, and he who sat on it had a bow; and a crown was given to him; and he went out conquering and to conquer" (Rev. 6:1-2).

The Significance of Daniel's Prophecy

At first, the Antichrist will pose as Israel's friend, and millions of Israelis will put their trust in him. But then, three and a half years later, his true character as Satan's masterpiece will be revealed. How can we understand this? Our Lord explained: "When you [Jewish disciples] see the ABOMI-NATION OF DESOLATION which was spoken of through Daniel the prophet, standing in the holy place (let the reader understand) ... then there will be a great tribulation such as has not occurred since the beginning of the world until now, nor ever will" (Matt. 24:15, 21). There it is! "Let the reader understand ... Daniel the prophet." What a tribute to that faithful servant of God who had died nearly six hundred years earlier! The Lord had told Daniel, "Seal up the book until the end of time ... knowledge will increase ... and none of the wicked will understand, but those who have insight will understand" (Dan. 12:4, 10). At this point we can truly identify with Daniel himself. With curiosity bordering on desperation, he cried out, "My lord, what will be the outcome of these events?" (Dan. 12:8). Fuller revelation was to come in the next four verses, as we shall see, and later through Haggai, Zechariah, and Malachi, and still later through the New Testament – especially the capstone of all prophecy, the book of Revelation. But the foundation of God's teaching concerning the final Antichrist was laid in the book of Daniel.

Let us say of Daniel's book what Peter said of Paul's letters: "Therefore, beloved, since you look for these things, be diligent to be found by Him in peace ... and regard the patience of our Lord as salvation; just as also our beloved brother Paul [and Daniel!], according to the wisdom given him, wrote to you, as also in all his letters, speaking in them of these things, in which are some things hard to understand, which the untaught and unstable distort, as they do also the rest of the Scriptures, to their own destruction" (2 Peter 3:14-16).

The Dragon of Isaiah 27

Nearly two hundred years before Daniel described the Antichrist, the greatest of all the writing prophets, Isaiah, was given a glimpse of this human "dragon." After describing the Great Tribulation (Isa. 26:20-21), he tells us that it will climax with the removal of Satan and his human agent, the Antichrist: "In that day the LORD will punish Leviathan the fleeing serpent [Satan] ... even Leviathan the twisted serpent; and He will kill the dragon who lives in the sea" (27:1).

Who is "the dragon who lives in the sea"? He is the "beast coming up out of the sea, having ten horns and seven heads," according to Revelation 13:1 – the Antichrist who emerges from the sea of humanity to rule the world under Satan for forty-two months (v. 5). Amazingly, "the dragon" of Isaiah 27 is the name given to Satan in Revelation 12 and 13! Their character is so similar that they both can share that image. To that extent, Antichrist can be called Satan incarnate!

The Little Horn of Daniel 7

Daniel, of course, knew and loved the writings of Isaiah, just as he knew and loved the book of Jeremiah (cf. Dan. 9:2). That helped him understand the identity, function, and destiny of the future Antichrist. One night, about 553 BC, God showed him "four great beasts … coming up from the sea [of humanity]." These were equivalent to the four great empires of Daniel 2 – Neo-Baylonia, Medo-Persia, Hellenistic Greece, and Rome (Dan. 7:3). Fifty years earlier, Daniel saw these empires as a gigantic humanlike statue made of beautiful metals, namely, gold, silver, bronze, and iron (2:32-33); but now he saw them as wild, ravenous beasts! How different are man's perspectives and God's perspective!

This time, the fourth kingdom, Rome, produces ten horns [i.e., kings], equivalent to the ten toes of chapter 2. But then, to our amazement, an eleventh horn appears! "Behold, another horn, a little one, came up among them, and … possessed eyes like the eyes of a man and a mouth uttering great boasts" (Dan. 7:8). This is a spectacular new element in predictive prophecy, only faintly hinted at in the writing prophets that preceded Daniel (Isa. 27:1, "the dragon who lives in the sea"). Christ and the apostles referred to this person as yet future to their own time (Matt. 24:5, 15; 2 Thess. 2:3-4; 1 John 2:18; 4:3; Rev. 13, 17, 19). The fact that he is said to come up "among" the ten horns indicates, therefore, that these horns (kings) are also yet future to the New Testament era. Frequently in the Old Testament the term *horn* is used to describe power, and thus, appropriately, powerful rulers (1 Kings 22:11; Ps. 75:10; 132:17; Zech. 1:18).

"Eyes like the eyes of a man" suggests great brilliance (cf. Ezek. 1; Zech. 3:9; 4:10); the "mouth uttering great boasts," in the light of later revelation, refers to blasphemous utterances

(7:25; Rev. 13:5-6). The combination of these two characteristics points to a man capable of incomparably brilliant blasphemies—not simply speaking against God but doing so in a manner that will attract and deceive vast numbers of people. Indeed, he will be Satan's masterpiece—a superbly effective instrument of "the father of lies," who was "a murderer from the beginning" (John 8:44).

Three of the first horns will be pulled out by the roots before it. The interpreting angel amplifies this statement in Daniel 7:20 ("before which three of them fell") and in verse 24 ("and will subdue three kings"). The threefold emphasis on this event (revealed nowhere else in prophetic Scripture) indicates a crucial means for Israel's future identification of the "little horn." Somehow, this powerful king will rise rapidly to international prominence by utterly crushing three of the ten kings who will already be on the scene (analogous to the three ribs in the mouth of the second beast, v. 5).

In Daniel 7:7-8 we see the frightful fourth beast with its blasphemous little horn. This is the devil at his worst. Then, with hardly a word of transition, the reader is hurried into the third heaven, into the very presence of God, where everything is under His absolutely sovereign control (v. 9). "He who sits in the heavens laughs, the Lord scoffs at them. Then He will speak to them in His anger and terrify them in His fury" (Ps. 2:4-5). The only possible outcome of this confrontation in a God-created, moral universe is utter and final divine judgment on every form of rebellion and wickedness.

Daniel wrote, "I kept looking ... until the beast was slain" (Dan. 7:11). A confrontation between the despicable fourth beast and the infinite Ancient of Days surely could not continue long in Daniel's vision. The fact that it continues for centuries in the real world is a major mystery in God's providential rule. The fiery destruction of the beast corresponds to the smashing of the image in Daniel 2 by means of the Stone from heaven (Rev. 19:20). In both cases, the end comes suddenly, supernaturally, and spectacularly.

"As for the rest of the beasts, their dominion was taken away, but an extension of life was granted to them for an appointed period of time" (Dan. 7:12). There is a significant contrast between the termination of the dominion of the fourth beast and that of the first three. Neo-Babylonia, Medo-Persia, and Greece were not totally destroyed when they lost their dominion but were largely merged into succeeding empires, so that elements of each still exist in the final phase of the Roman kingdom.[1] Totally different, however, will be the fate of the fourth kingdom at the Second Coming. Nothing of it will be left to contaminate Christ's millennial kingdom. Then, and then only, will God smash the kingdoms of this world. They "became like chaff from the summer threshing floors; and the wind carried them away so that not a trace of them was found" (Dan. 2:35).[2]

Christ and the Antichrist

Daniel was greatly "distressed" by all of this and wrote, "The visions in my mind kept alarming me" (Dan. 7:15). But everything was, is, and always will be under God's total control! Daniel wrote, "I kept looking in the night visions, and behold, with the clouds of heaven One like a Son of Man [the preincarnate Christ] was coming, and He came up to the Ancient of Days [God the Father] and was presented before

---

[1] See John C. Whitcomb, *Daniel* (Chicago: Moody, 1985), 47, commenting on Daniel 2:35.

[2] John F. Walvoord, *Daniel: The Key to Prophetic Revelation* (Chicago: Moody, 1971), 166.

Him. And to Him [Christ] was given dominion, glory and a kingdom ... which will not be destroyed" (vv. 13-14).

We praise God for this assurance! The Antichrist, Satan's masterpiece, will rule the world for forty-two months (Dan. 9:27; Rev. 13:5-18). During those three and a half years, he will even be allowed by God to overpower, "wear down ... overcome" God's people (Dan. 7:21, 25; Rev. 13:7). But then, at Christ's second coming, at Armageddon, "his dominion will be taken away, annihilated and destroyed forever" (Dan. 7:26; cf. Rev. 19:19-20).

That is only one small part of what our Lord meant when He commanded us to pray: "Our Father which art in heaven, Hallowed be thy name. Thy kingdom come. Thy will be done in earth, as it is in heaven" (Matt. 6:9-10 KJV). May that prayer be ours each day we live – until He comes!

Daniel and the Rise of the Antichrist

Daniel then approached "one of those who were standing by and began asking him the exact meaning of all this" (Dan. 7:16). We may be profoundly grateful that Daniel was not satisfied with his visionary prophetic lesson that night. He had an insatiable desire for more and more explanations and interpretations of God's infinitely precious Word, and therefore more truth was given to him and to us by the interpreting angel. How much of His Word would never have been revealed if (on the purely human level) Christ's disciples had never asked questions of their Lord! God invites us to ask Him for wisdom in the interpretation of His Word (James 1:5), with the understanding that He is not obliged to reveal to us all of His "secret things" (Deut. 29:29; John 16:12). Nevertheless, many of God's servants would give a great deal to stand, as it were, in Daniel's shoes and to ask an angelic interpreter "the exact meaning of all this"!

The interpreting angel explained, "Four kings ... will arise from the earth. But the saints of the Highest One will receive the kingdom and possess the kingdom forever" (Dan. 7:17-18). The angel very briefly pointed to two key ideas. First, these beasts represent human kings and their kingdoms (2:37-44). Second, their dominions will not last forever but will be replaced by God's kingdom, governed through His people, which will indeed continue forever (2:44).

Daniel particularly wanted "to know the exact meaning of the fourth beast ... the ten horns that were on its head, and the other horn which came up" (7:19-20). Because of the similarity of this vision to the one he had interpreted for Nebuchadnezzar a half century earlier, Daniel may have surmised the two key ideas that the angel gave him. Biblical revelation does follow consistent patterns, even in eschatology, so that the careful and reverent interpreter need not be totally frustrated, even by the use of symbolic language.

Encouraged now by the willingness of the angel to help him, Daniel boldly asked for more particulars on the dreadful fourth beast (with "claws of bronze" — a new detail) and its ten horns, but especially that "other horn which came up ... which was larger in appearance than its associates." But before waiting for the angel's answer, he had to continue describing the fascinating outcome of the great conflict to reassure himself (and us) that however dreadful the earthly kingdoms might be in their wickedness, God is sovereign in the universe, and His mighty program will finally prevail through His people, to whom victory will come in spite of the apparent "overpowering" war waged against them by the little horn (cf. Ps. 110:1-3).

Realizing that Daniel was particularly fascinated by the eleventh horn, the angel hurried through his explanation of the fourth beast and its ten horns and focused on the eleventh, saying, "And another will arise after them, and he will be different from the previous ones and will subdue three kings" (Dan. 7:24). Here the angel revealed a new truth concerning the eleventh horn: it "will arise after" the first ten. It cannot be long after, for Daniel had already seen that it "came up among them" (7:8). Thus, this final king, contemporary with the ten, not only arises after the first ten (thus the title, "a little one," 7:8) but finally, through his sudden and spectacular conquests of three of the ten (cf. 7:8, 20), looms "larger in appearance than its associates" (7:20) and thus becomes amazingly "different from the previous ones." This is the Antichrist of 2 Thessalonians 2, 1 John 2 and 4, and the book of Revelation.

The New Testament does not emphasize the initial phase of the career of the final Antichrist. He appears there as the ruler of the entire world (e.g., Matt. 24; 2 Thess. 2; Rev. 11, 13, 17), with his "deadly wound" already healed by bodily resuscitation (Rev. 13:3, 12, 14). On the basis of chronological comparison (see Dan. 9:27), we may designate Daniel 7:24 as the first half of the seventieth "week" of Daniel 9, a three-and-one-half-year period immediately following the removal of the Church from the world (Rev. 3:10), during which time God will begin His final program of discipline and indoctrination and preparation of Israel for her official function as witnesses to the true God. Although the nation of Israel is still largely apostate during this earlier period, the two special witnesses of God will be carrying on their great work in Jerusalem (Rev. 11:3-13), even while the "little horn" grows rapidly in power among the ten kings and continues his covenant relationship with Israel (Dan. 9:27).[3]

---

[3] See chapter 5 for more on the chronology of this period, as well as the chart at the end of this chapter.

The little horn, the Antichrist, "will speak out against the Most High" (Dan. 7:25). This is now the second half of the seventieth week of Daniel 9, a forty-two-month period that begins with Antichrist's rising from the dead, killing the two witnesses (Rev. 11:7), breaking his covenant with Israel (Dan. 9:27), setting up (through the False Prophet) an image of himself in the Jerusalem temple to be worshipped by all mankind (Matt. 24:15; 2 Thess. 2:3-4; Rev. 13:11-17), and spewing forth incomparably brilliant blasphemies against the living God. These ultimate blasphemies involve the demand that people worship him and a fallen angel (Satan) who strengthens him (Rev. 13:2, 4-6, 14-15). Through the ages, Satan, "the god of this world," has desperately desired that all human beings, bearing the image of God, should worship him (Matt. 4:9-10; cf. Gen. 3:1-5). This will be his supreme opportunity, but he knows "that he has only a short time" (Rev. 12:12).

The Antichrist will "wear down the saints of the Highest One" (Dan. 7:25). This theme of the sufferings of Israelite believers during their future time of great tribulation is introduced here (and 7:21) in the book of Daniel for the first time, though it will be emphasized increasingly toward the end of the book (8:24; 9:26; 11:32-35; 12:10). Moses had predicted this in general terms (Lev. 26; Deut. 28). Isaiah had spoken about it as a great purging time (4:3-4), and Jeremiah as "the time of Jacob's distress" (30:7). See also Ezekiel 20, Zechariah 12, and Malachi 3. So devastating will be that final phase of "the day of man" that two-thirds of the nation of Israel will die and, the Lord "will bring the third part through the fire" (Zech. 13:9; cf. Isa. 6:13). Israel's Messiah assured her that "then there will be a great tribulation, such as has not occurred since the beginning of the world until now, nor ever will" (Matt. 24:21). In fact, unless those days are "cut short," none will survive at all, "but for the sake of the elect those days will be cut short" (Matt 24:22).

Prophetic Scripture emphasizes the extreme plight of God's people at the hand of the Antichrist at that time, so that he is actually given authority "to make war with the saints and to overcome them" (Rev. 13:7; cf. Dan. 7:21). Just at the time the forces of evil are ready to destroy Jerusalem, the last stronghold of the saints, "the Lord will go forth and fight against those nations" (Zech. 14:1-3), and the remnant will be rescued. Large numbers of Israelites will already have fled to the wilderness regions (Rev. 12:13-16), as Jesus advised (Matt. 24:15-20), and 144,000 others, sealed by God from death (though not from extreme suffering, Matt. 25:35-40), will carry "this gospel of the kingdom" to "the whole world as a testimony to all the nations, and then the end will come" (Matt. 24:14; Rev. 7:1-8).

The Antichrist "will intend to make alterations in times and in law" (Dan. 7:25). In context, this seems to refer to divine "time" and "law." Satan will know that his "time" is short (Rev. 12:12), but his human instrument (like Hitler, who planned a one-thousand-year kingdom) will doubtless intend to extend the "time" allotted to him in Scripture (Daniel and Revelation) forever. He will learn, however, that his days will decline "in [the Lord's] fury," and he will finish his years "like a sigh" (Ps. 90:9), for only God is "from everlasting to everlasting" (Ps. 90:2).

The "law" he will intend to change probably will be the law of God. One law of God is that "the soul who sins will die" (Ezek. 18:4, 20; Rom. 6:23). The Antichrist, speaking for the "father of lies," will seek to reverse this foundational law of the moral and spiritual universe, just as Satan said to Eve: "You surely will not die!" (Gen. 3:4). God pronounces "woe to those who call evil good, and good evil; who substitute darkness for light and light for darkness" (Isa. 5:20). The Antichrist will indeed be "the man of lawlessness" (2 Thess. 2:3) and will culminate the desire of fallen men throughout history to cast off every divine restraint that has been imposed upon the world for man's good (Ps. 2:1-3).

"They will be given into his hand for a time, times, and half a time" (Dan. 7:25). Since this final period of Israel's testing is said to last for 1,260 days (Rev. 11:3; 12:6), which is forty-two months (Rev. 13:5), three and a half years (half of the seven-year covenant period, Dan. 9:27), "time" must be one year, "times" must be two years, and "half a time" must be half a year—thus, three and one-half years. The same expression appears in 12:7. (On this basis, it may be assumed that the seven "times" God pronounced upon Nebuchadnezzar were likewise years; 4:16, 25, 32.) The amazing conquests of such militarists as Alexander, Napoleon, and Hitler will all be completely eclipsed by the global dominion of the Antichrist. As God prepared Israel for the brightness of David by the darkness of Saul, so also, on a vastly greater scale, the ultimate hour of darkness of our invisible enemy (John 12:31) will be overwhelmed by "the sun of righteousness" which "will rise with healing in its wings" (Mal. 4:2).

Then "his dominion will be taken away, annihilated and destroyed forever" (Dan. 7:26). The thoroughness of the Antichrist's destruction here parallels the effect of the crushing Stone of Daniel 2 (cf. Zech. 11:17). The New Testament confirms this vision, for "that lawless one" will be slain "with the breath of His mouth" and will be brought "to an end by the appearance of His coming" (2 Thess. 2:8). Furthermore, he and his False Prophet will be "thrown alive into the lake of fire which burns with brimstone" (Rev. 19:20), and, together with the "father" of this unholy trio, Satan himself, "they will be tormented day and night forever and ever" (Rev. 20:10).

"Then the sovereignty, the dominion and the greatness of all the kingdoms under the whole heaven will be given to the people of the saints of the Highest One" (Dan. 7:27). This clarification of 7:22 must also be harmonized with the promise that the everlasting kingdom will be given to Christ (7:13-14). The Son of Man graciously shares His dominion with His blood-bought children. The marvelous promise that God gives to His people is that "if we endure, we will also reign with Him" (2 Tim. 2:12). Isaiah saw the day when the spoils of victory would be divided by the Messiah with His people, called, by His grace, "the great" and "the strong" (Isa. 53:12). In light of this, Paul insisted that "the sufferings of this present time are not worthy to be compared with the glory that is to be revealed to us" (Rom. 8:18). And John tells us that shortly after the destruction of the Antichrist at the second coming of Christ, "I saw thrones, and ... the souls of those who had been beheaded because of their testimony of Jesus ... and they came to life and ... will be priests of God and of Christ and will reign with Him for a thousand years" (Rev. 20:4, 6). God's people in the midst of intense suffering for Him will never be disappointed in their hope of reigning with Him, for such hope is God's means of giving us maturity (Rom. 5:3-5).

The King of the North and the Antichrist

Now, we have seen that the Antichrist, "the prince who is to come" (Dan. 9:26-27), will break his seven-year covenant with Israel, will "put a stop to sacrifice and grain offering" in the temple, and will set up an "abomination of desolation" for forty-two months (9:27; 11:31). But how does all this come about? God told Daniel that this satanic monster "will do as he pleases, and he will exalt and magnify himself above every god and will speak monstrous things against the God of gods"

(11:36). In contrast to Antiochus Epiphanes, who was a relatively minor "King of the North,"[4] this king will attempt to control both the bodies and the souls of all human beings on earth. Satanic pride and blasphemy, shockingly present in Antiochus, will reach their ultimate expression in this "willful king" (from KJV, "the king shall do according to his will"). He is surely the final Antichrist of 1 John 2:18a and 4:3, because "the beast" that dominates the central section of John's final book (Rev. 11–13, 17) fits not only the description of Daniel 11:36-39 but also the picture of the "little horn" of Daniel 7:25 (including the chronological framework). From this point in Daniel's final vision to the ultimate and incomparable "time of distress" (12:1), this Roman "beast out of the sea" comes into focus either explicitly (11:36-39) or implicitly (11:40, 44-45; 12:1). What Antiochus Epiphanes foreshadowed, he embodies.

Daniel tells us the Antichrist "will prosper until the indignation is finished, for that which is decreed will be done" (11:36). The shocking challenge to God's sovereignty that people will see in this depraved world ruler calls for clear reminders that evil is not only temporarily tolerated by God but is actually included in His decree (cf. Gen. 45:5, 7; 50:20). Two years earlier, Daniel had been told in similar terms that God would accomplish His purposes through this wicked one "even until a complete destruction, one that is decreed, is poured out on the one who makes desolate" (9:27). Thus, a recurring theme of the book of Daniel is the absolute sovereignty of God in the midst of human and angelic rebellion (cf. Dan. 4:17, 25).

---

[4] Antiochus, a Seleucid ruler of the second century BC, was one of history's greatest persecutors of Israel. He is described prophetically in Daniel 8:9 as a "rather small horn" and in 11:21 as a "despicable person." See Whitcomb, *Daniel*, 111-19.

Daniel 11:37 says of this coming ruler, "He will show no regard for the gods [God] of his fathers." Will the Antichrist be a Jew? In Revelation 13:1 he is described as "a beast coming up out of the sea," which symbolizes the Gentile world (cf. Dan. 7:2-3; Rev. 17:15). But he could be a Jew born and raised in a Gentile nation and still fit this description. An even more important question is how apostate Israel will view this person. If they see him as their Messiah, they would more likely accept him as such if he were a Jew (Deut. 18:15, 18; 2 Sam. 7:12). But it is not altogether clear they will see him as their true Messiah at the time they enter into the seven-year covenant (Dan. 9:27), unless our Lord implied this in John 5:43 (cf. Matt. 24:5). A key question is whether *'elohîm* at the beginning of 11:37 is to be understood as singular ("God") or plural ("gods"), for "the God of his fathers" would indicate that he is a Jew. The Hebrew wording in the following verse ("instead," or lit., "in his place") suggests a singular antecedent. Edward J. Young concludes: "The phrase has a Jewish emphasis and has reference to the Jewish religion. The one who has no regard for this Jewish religion is himself a Jew, the Antichrist. I fully agree with Gaebelein's statement, 'Here his Jewish descent becomes evident.'"[5]

Neither shall the Antichrist have regard for "the desire of women." "He shall set himself free ... from all piety toward men and God, from all the tender affections of the love of men and of God. The 'love of women' [cf. 2 Sam. 1:26] is named as an example ... of that affection of human love and attachment

---

[5] Edward J. Young, *The Prophecy of Daniel* (Grand Rapids: Eerdmans, 1949), 249. See A. C. Gaebelein, *The Prophet Daniel* (New York: Our Hope, 1911), 188.

for which even the most selfish and most savage of men feel some sensibility."[6]

Furthermore, "he will honor a god of fortresses … he will give great honor to those who acknowledge him" (Dan. 11:38-39). The Antichrist will lavish all his vast resources upon military fortifications and programs and will encourage cooperation by distributing positions of authority and valuable property to his followers.

Daniel 11:40 states, "And at the end time the king of the South will collide with him, and the king of the North will storm against him … and he will enter countries, overflow them, and pass through." "At the end time" is a clear eschatological reference in the book of Daniel (cf. 11:35; 12:4, 9). The King of the South must therefore be a yet future Egyptian monarch, judging from the previous use of the term in this chapter and also the clear statements of 11:42-43. Presumably in alliance with a King of the North (such as Russia today?), the eschatological Egyptian ruler will launch a diversionary thrust and "will collide with him," that is, with "the king [who] will do as he pleases" (the Antichrist) in the immediately preceding context (11:36-39).

It is important to note that the antecedent of "him" (used twice in verse 40) must be the Antichrist, whose location at this time will be somewhere between the "north" and the "south," presumably Palestine.

Could the King of the North be Syria? No, for his "attack on Antichrist involves the King of the North's entering, overflowing, and passing through other countries en route to Pal-

---

[6] C. F. Keil, *Biblical Commentary on the Book of Daniel* (1872; reprint, Grand Rapids: Eerdmans, 1955), 465. For a discussion of other possible interpretations of this difficult expression, see Walvoord, *Daniel*, 274-75.

estine."[7] The name of any particular "King of the North" may indeed change with the flux of history, but the general location remains fixed. "Russia meets the hermeneutical requirements involved in the title 'King of the North' associated with the Seleucid empire [of vv. 5-29]. It has a corresponding northern location, a corresponding vast geographical scope, and a corresponding vast political preeminence."[8]

Although agreeing that three distinct kings are seen in Daniel 11:40-45, most premillennialists understand the pronoun *he* in these verses to refer to the Antichrist, not the King of the North. Thus, when the King of the Sorth storms against him with chariots, horsemen, and many ships, the Antichrist is viewed as launching a counterattack whereby "he will enter countries." This great conflict is seen as continuing throughout the last half of the Seventieth Week until the Antichrist comes to supernatural judgment at Armageddon.[9]

Among the difficulties with this view are: (1) Revelation 13:4 seems to contradict the idea that the Antichrist will require forty-two months to subdue his enemies; (2) the "rumors" he hears are from Palestine ("the Beautiful Land"), east and north of Libya and Ethiopia, not from the Euphrates River as generally understood (cf. Rev. 16:12); (3) if the king in 11:45 were the Antichrist, 12:1 would seem to be anticlimactic, whereas the Antichrist is the climax of all evil forces until the second coming of Christ; (4) it is not primarily Israel, but rath-

---

[7] George M. Harton, "An Interpretation of Daniel 11:36-45," *Grace Theological Journal* 4, no. 2 (Fall 1983): 214.

[8] Ibid.

[9] Ibid., 216. For an exposition of the majority view among premillennial scholars, see J. Dwight Pentecost, *Things to Come* (Grand Rapids: Zondervan, 1958), 356.

er the Antichrist, who is attacked by both the King of the South and the King of the North in this passage.[10]

How does the Antichrist finally attain global authority? The clue comes from Revelation 13 and 17: "his fatal wound was healed" (13:3, 12, 14; cf. 17:8, 11). This thrice-repeated statement presupposes an interpretation of Daniel 11:40-45 that sees the Antichrist ("the king who does as he pleases," 11:36-39) killed by the irresistible King of the North, sweeping through countries in his southward thrust into "the Beautiful Land."

The entire passage (Daniel 11:40-45) describing the King of the North thus constitutes a parenthetical background explanation of the stupendous rise of the Antichrist to world supremacy after both the King of the North and the King of the South are removed as threats to his demonic and blasphemous ambitions (cf. Gen. 11:1-9 as a similar parenthetical flashback into Gen. 10). The invasion of Palestine by the King of the North probably occurs only a few months before the events of Revelation 13 (and Dan. 11:36-39; 12:1) and provides the background for them.

"The king of the North will storm against him with chariots, with horsemen, and with many ships" (11:40). Note the threefold emphasis on irresistible military power, and compare with Ezekiel 38:9 ("you will come like a storm … like a cloud covering the land [of Israel]").

"He will also enter the Beautiful Land, and many countries will fall; but these will be rescued out of his hand: Edom, Moab and the foremost of the sons of Ammon" (Dan. 11:41). Entering Palestine from the far north (passing through "countries" to get there), the King of the North rushes southward into Africa so rapidly that he doesn't even take time to con-

---

[10] Harton, "An Interpretation of Daniel 11:36-45," 220.

quer the trans-Jordan areas of Edom, Moab, and Ammon (see Isa. 11:14 for Israel's ultimate conquest of these territories). "Then he will stretch out his hand against other countries, and the land of Egypt will not escape" (11:42). The King of the North apparently has no great concern for possible flank attacks on his extended lines of communication with his now far-distant homeland, for the Antichrist has presumably been killed with the sword of the King of the North (cf. 11:40, "he will … overflow them, and pass through"; Rev. 13:14). Totally ignoring the alliance with the King of the South, which presumably served as the mechanism for a great pincer attack on the Antichrist, the King of the North now conquers his former ally! One does not need to look far for contemporary examples of such international treachery.

As a result, "he will gain control over the hidden treasures of gold and silver, and over all the precious things of Egypt; and Libyans and Ethiopians will follow at his heels" (Dan. 11:43). In that day, as to some extent today, Egypt (King of the South) may be allied with oil-rich Arab nations and thus, in spite of the presence of an impoverished lower class, will be irresistibly attractive to the King of the North (cf. Ezek. 38:13 for Gog's grasp after silver and gold).

Having destroyed the King of the South and occupying his Egyptian domain, the King of the North now sends his victorious armies westward into Libya and further southward into Ethiopia. Compare Ezekiel 38:5. With all of northeast Africa within his grasp, he seems to be on his way to achieving world dominion. But then, a totally unexpected and electrifying event occurs that eventuates in his complete destruction.

"Rumors from the East and from the North will disturb him, and he will go forth with great wrath to destroy and annihilate many. He will pitch the tents of his royal pavilion between the seas and the beautiful Holy Mountain; yet he will come to his end, and no one will help him" (11:44-45). Many have understood "the East" to refer to "the kings of the east" coming to the battle of Armageddon (Rev. 16:12). But the battle of Armageddon occurs at the end of the Seventieth Week, and these events occur just before the middle of the seven-year period (cf. Dan. 12:1). Furthermore, the fact that "the East" and "the North" point to Palestine as seen from Africa is confirmed by the movement of the King of the North back to "the beautiful Holy Mountain" (i.e., Jerusalem) rather than to regions to the east of Palestine.

But what are these "rumors" that "disturb" him to such an extent that he abandons his entire African campaign and is compelled to "go forth with great wrath to destroy and annihilate many" and to spread out his vast army "between the seas [the Dead Sea and the Mediterranean] and the beautiful Holy Mountain"?

Various prophetic indicators (e.g., Dan. 9:27; Matt. 24:15; 2 Thess. 2:3-4; Rev. 11:13, 17) focus our attention upon an event of almost cosmic significance that God directs Satan to accomplish in Jerusalem at the mid-point of the Seventieth Week, three and one-half years before the second coming of Christ: (1) The Antichrist receives "the wound of the sword," which kills him (Rev. 13:14; cf. 13:3, 12); (2) he thus enters into the realm of the dead and "is not" (Rev. 17:8, 11); (3) he then is enabled "to come up out of the abyss" (Rev. 11:7; 17:8) to begin a second earthly, nonglorified life as the eighth and greatest enemy of Israel (having previously been the seventh, Rev. 17:10-11); (4) he immediately kills God's two witnesses (Rev. 11:7), suggesting that his death and return to life occur in Jerusalem; (5) the False Prophet then erects an image of the Antichrist (Matt. 24:15, "the ABOMINATION OF DESOLATION ... standing in the holy place"), is enabled to give it the breath of life and the power to kill all opponents (Rev. 13:14-

15), insists that the Antichrist is God almighty (2 Thess. 2:4), and brings down fire from heaven to demonstrate it (Rev. 13:13); (6) the Antichrist breaks his seven-year covenant with Israel (Dan. 9:27) and begins a forty-two-month persecution of the believing remnant of Israel (Rev. 12:6, "the woman fled into the wilderness … one thousand two hundred and sixty days").

The detailed scenario of prophetic events surrounding the beginning of the final phase of the Antichrist's career on earth points back to and presupposes the destruction of his ultimate earthly enemy. This enemy is not described in the New Testament because ample information is provided in Daniel 11:40-45, which in turn builds upon Ezekiel 38–39 (Gog from Magog).

But even Gog was not a new figure in Old Testament prophecy: "Thus says the Lord God, 'Are you the one of whom I spoke in former days through My servants the prophets of Israel, who prophesied in those days for many years that I would bring you against them?'" (Ezek. 38:17). Looking farther back along the line of progressive revelation, we find Joel speaking of the fate of a great "northern army," which will do "great things" and yet will be destroyed between Palestine's "eastern sea" and "western sea" (Joel 2:20). Isaiah and Micah, in the late eighth century BC, saw this one as "the Assyrian," using the name of a familiar northern military power as a contemporary analogy for the final "King of the North" (Isa. 10:12, 24-27; Mic. 5:5-6).[11]

Now where are the connections between the Old Testament prophetic picture of the destruction of the great King of the North and the rise of the Antichrist who will overcome the

---

[11] See William F. Foster, "The Eschatological Significance of the Assyrian in the Old Testament" (Th.D. diss., Grace Theological Seminary, 1956).

saints (Dan. 7:21; Rev. 13:7) and gain control of the entire earth (Rev. 13:7, 8)?

One clear connection is the destruction of the King of the North (i.e., Gog) by fire from heaven, as described by Ezekiel: "I will rain on him and on his troops ... a torrential rain, with hailstones, fire and brimstone ... on the mountains of Israel" (Ezek. 38:22; 39:4). This supernatural destruction by fire (cf. Exod. 9:23-24) will either be indirectly delegated by God to Satan (cf. Job 1:12, 16) or will be accomplished directly. In either case, the False Prophet performs a similar miracle (Rev. 13:13), perhaps claiming that he, through Satan, had thus destroyed the great northern army in the land of Israel, leaving the Beast/Antichrist in full control of the world.

Another close connection between the Old Testament and the New Testament in this crucial event is the return of the Roman "Beast" from the realm of the dead. It will be on this basis that "the whole earth" will be "amazed," will follow "after the beast" (Rev. 13:3), and will ask, "Who is like the beast, and who is able to wage war with him?" (Rev. 13:4). It seems rather obvious that the Beast/Antichrist is killed by some great king in a battle (Rev. 13:14, "the wound of the sword"), comes back to life (Rev. 13:3, 12, 14), and then somehow destroys (or at least claims to have destroyed) his mighty enemy so that all mankind trembles before him. What great enemy could this be, if it is not the "northern army" of Joel, the eschatological Assyrian of Isaiah and Micah, and the Gog of Ezekiel? This is the King of the North in Daniel 11:40-45, who defeats the willful king of Daniel 11:36-39 and who, in turn, mysteriously "will come to his end" so that "no one will help him" just before Israel enters into "a time of distress such as never occurred since there was a nation until that time" (Dan. 12:1).

Thus the great King of the North passes off the scene by the midpoint of the Seventieth Week and serves New Testament eschatology only as a necessary backdrop or launching pad for the Antichrist, the ultimate masterpiece of Satan. The King of the North will be the inflictor of the "fatal wound" upon this Beast and thus will prove to be the greatest military challenge on earth for the false christ who gallops forth in the beginning of the Seventieth Week, "conquering and to conquer" (Rev. 6:2). By carefully comparing Scripture with Scripture, Old Testament with New Testament, this highly complex phase of end-time events gradually takes shape in the mind's eye of the student of God's prophetic Word.[12]

Michael, Satan, and the Antichrist

"At that time Michael, the great prince [archangel] who stands guard over the sons of your people [Israel], will arise" (Dan. 12:1). If the events of 11:40-45 reach their climax at the middle of the Seventieth Week, we would expect Michael to "arise" also "at that time." This seems to be confirmed by Revelation 12:7-12, which dates the final victory of Michael over Satan 1,260 days (12:6), or three and one-half "times" (12:14), before the second coming of Christ.

If Israel needed Michael's help in the days of Daniel (cf. Dan. 10:13, 21), she shall need it even more in her final great tribulation, for that "will be a time of distress such as never occurred since there was a nation until that time" (12:1). Previous revelation (e.g., Dan. 7:21, 25; 8:23-25; 9:27) and later revelation (e.g., Zech. 11:15-17; Matt. 24:15-24; 2 Thess. 2:3-4; Rev. 13) emphasize not only the time period of special distress for Israel that is coming but also the horrible visible instrument of that distress, the Antichrist. Thus, the willful king of

---

[12] See Paul Lee Tan, *The Interpretation of Prophecy* (Dallas: Bible Communications, 2001), 347; and *Jesus Is Coming* (Rockville, MD: Assurance Publishers, 1982), 64.

Daniel 11:36-39, the final victor against the King of the North in 11:45, becomes the ultimate persecutor of Michael's people, Israel.[13]

Under God, Michael, the archangel, is the key person for Israel's destiny. For thousands of years, God has used him to fight against Satan and his demons (Dan. 10:13, 21), just as He uses the Church today (cf. Eph. 6:12). When Israel rejected her Messiah, however, Michael and Israel were temporarily set aside (cf. Rom. 11:11-25). But when the Church is raptured to heaven, "the voice of the archangel" will be heard again (1 Thess. 4:16)! Forty-two months later, he and his angels will finally be enabled by God to cast Satan out of the gateway to heaven, where he has been accusing the saints "before our God day and night" (Rev. 12:10; cf. Job 1:9-11; Zech. 3:1).

When Satan is cast down to the earth, the Great Tribulation begins: "Woe to the earth and the sea, because the devil has come down to you, having great wrath, knowing that he has only a short time" (Rev. 12:12). Amazingly, God will allow him to raise the Antichrist from the dead (cf. Rev. 11:7; 17:8-11) and give him global dominion; "and the dragon [Satan] [will give] him his power and his throne and great authority" (Rev. 13:2). The way is now clear for the Antichrist to rule the entire world. Yet Michael will arise and from this time of great distress Israel "will be rescued" (Dan. 12:1; cf. Matt. 24:22).

Would not Daniel have been amazed to read this capstone to all the Bible – the book of Revelation? Yes! But one thing he fully understood: the Lord will bring final victory to His persecuted people. "The court will sit for judgment, and his dominion will be taken away, annihilated and destroyed forever. Then the sovereignty, the dominion, and the greatness of all the kingdoms under the whole heaven will be given to the

---

[13] Harton, "An Interpretation of Daniel 11:36-45," 230.

people of the saints of the Highest One; His kingdom will be an everlasting kingdom, and all the dominions will serve and obey Him" (Dan. 7:26-27).

Darkness before the Dawn

Over and over again, God told Daniel that the "saints of the Highest One" (Jewish believers and their Gentile converts) will be crushed by the Antichrist (the "little horn" of Daniel 7 and "the king [who] will do as he pleases" of Daniel 11:36). They will be overpowered (7:21) and worn down (7:25a), and "they will be given into his hand" (7:25b). This was very hard on Daniel – and should be on us! The prophet wrote, "As for me, Daniel, my thoughts were greatly alarming me and my face grew pale" (7:28). But, thank God, the spiritual darkness of the Great Tribulation will soon be followed by the Light of the World, our Lord Jesus Christ, who will rescue His people and inaugurate the kingdom! Someone has said that the darkness is deepest just before the dawn. And so shall it be at the Second Coming.

The Great Tribulation

But how long will this time of incomparable global darkness continue? Daniel heard two angels ask the Lord, "How long will it be until the end of these wonders?" (Dan. 12:6). The answer? It will be "for a time, times, and half a time; and as soon as they finish shattering the power of the holy people, all these events will be completed" (12:7). That means three and one-half years, as explained in Daniel 9:24-27 and in Revelation 11:2-3. This will be the last half of the seven-year Tribulation period that follows the resurrection/rapture of the Church and ends with the glorious second coming of Christ.

Daniel's last question would surely be ours as well: "O, my lord, what shall be the end of these things?" (Dan. 12:8 KJV). God's answer: "Many [saints] will be purged, purified and refined, but the wicked [especially Antichrist] will act wickedly, and none of the wicked will understand" (12:10).

The 1,290 Days and the 1,335 Days

Now comes a special revelation, taught nowhere else in the Bible! After Antichrist sets up his "abomination of desolation" in the middle of that seven-year period (cf. Dan. 9:27; Matt. 24:15-22), "there will be 1,290 days" (Dan. 12:11). We know that the Lord will return 1,260 days later (Rev. 12:6; 13:5). Instead of twelve hundred and SIXTY days, however, we are told that there will be twelve hundred and NINETY days! Could the answer be that the Lord will set aside those THIRTY days to purge and purify the temple for His people to use during the kingdom age? Godly King Hezekiah postponed the Passover one month in order to cleanse the temple and to consecrate the priesthood because of the abominations committed by his father Ahaz (2 Chron. 29–30). "Likewise, Judas Maccabaeus and his army went to great lengths to cleanse the Jerusalem Temple of the abominations of Antiochus Epiphanes in 164 B.C."[14]

But now, the last detail: "How blessed is he who keeps waiting and attains to the 1,335 days!" (Dan. 12:12). Here is another FORTY-FIVE days! Before the kingdom can officially begin, all unbelievers must be removed. How awesome! When the 371 days of the Genesis Flood finally ended, only believers were alive! Indeed, as our Lord explained, "They [unbelievers]

---

[14] Whitcomb, *Daniel*, 168.

did not understand until the flood came and took them all away; so shall the coming of the Son of Man be" (Matt. 24:39).

The very first to be removed from the world will be the Antichrist and his demonic team at Armageddon (Rev. 19:17–20:3). Then, the unbelieving leaders of all Gentile nations – "the goats" (Matt. 25:31-46; cf. Joel 3:1-3) – will be removed. Then, any Jews who are still "rebels" (Ezek. 20:33-38; Mal. 3:1-6) will be taken away. And finally, by the 1,335th day, any man "in the field" and any woman "grinding at the mill" who still rejects the Savior "will be taken [to judgment]" (Matt. 24:40-41; Luke 17:34-35) – the opposite of what will happen at the rapture of the Church seven years earlier! Thus, what the Lord Jesus Christ said will be finally accomplished: "the one who endures to the end [1,335 days after Antichrist's great blasphemy], he will be saved" (Matt. 24:13). Daniel had heard enough: "the wicked [especially Antichrist] will act wickedly," but, praise God, "those who have insight will understand" (Dan. 12:10). Darkness before the dawn! Antichrist, yes. But then the true Christ! The Father will give Him AN EVER-LASTING DOMINION WHICH WILL NOT PASS AWAY!

AMEN! THANK YOU, GOD!

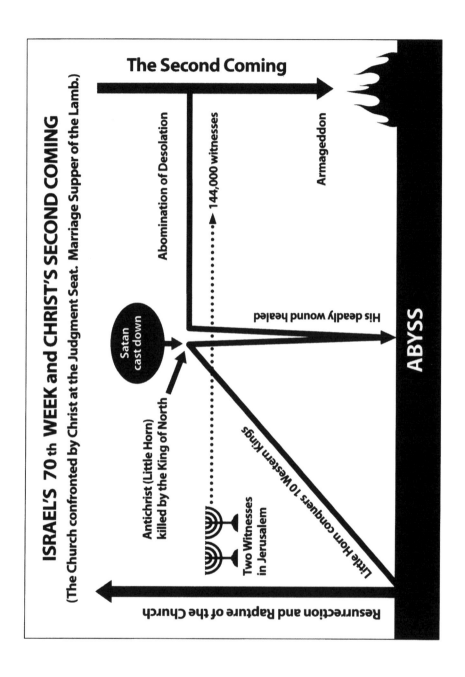

7

The Two Witnesses of Revelation 11

The Time of Their Ministry

Most dispensational commentators agree that the holy city, Jerusalem, will be "trodden down" by the Gentiles for forty-two months *during the last half of the Seventieth Week of Daniel* (Rev. 11:2, cf. Luke 21:24). This time period is identical to the forty-two months of Revelation 13:5, which is the time God assigns to the Beast, or Antichrist, to blaspheme God's name and to persecute His people.

This will be the fulfillment of Daniel's prophecy in Daniel 7:21, that "the little horn" will make war against the saints and will prevail against them until "the Ancient of Days" finally comes (v. 22). Daniel is also told that "the saints shall be given into his hand for a time and times and half a time" (v. 25), and that after these three and one-half years, "when the power of the holy people has been completely shattered, all these things shall be finished" (12:7).[1]

What, then, are the "one thousand two hundred and sixty days" during which "my two witnesses" will receive authority to "prophesy ... clothed in sackcloth" (Rev. 11:3)? Time

---

[1] Scripture quotations in this chapter are from the NKJV.

107

indicators, such as "1,260 days" are to be understood literally. John F. Walvoord explains: "Very prominent in the book of Revelation is the use of numbers, namely, 2, 3, 3½, 4, 5, 6, 7, 10, 12, 24, 42, 144, 666, 1,000, 1,260, 1,600, 7,000, 12,000, 144,000, 100,000,000, 200,000,000 ... The general rule should be followed to interpret numbers literally unless there is clear evidence to the contrary."[2]

For several reasons, I suggest that the 1,260 days *is the first half of the Seventieth Week. First,* there seems to be an intentional distinction between the time of the Gentile occupation of the temple's outer court and the city and the time of the two witnesses, indicated by the different time units used: 42 months for the Gentile domination and 1,260 days for the two witnesses. If the same time period is intended for both groups, why is not the 42-month time block sufficient to cover both?

Second, and more important, in the very next verse (Rev. 11:4), the ministry of the two witnesses is compared to the ministry of the two olive trees of Zechariah 4:3, namely *Joshua* the high priest and *Zerubbabel* the governor of the Jewish remnant, who returned from Babylon to reestablish legitimate worship in Jerusalem (Zech. 3:1; 4:6). *These leaders did not have to wait for the temple to be rebuilt to begin sacrificing on the altar they erected on the ruins of Solomon's temple* (cf. Ezra 3:2-3). *By the same token, the two witnesses will not have to wait for the third temple to be built in order to begin sacrificing on a divinely legitimate altar on the present ruins of the second temple.* What they *will* need is supernatural protection to reinstitute the sacrifices (cf. Dan. 9:27) in the presence of enormous, even global, opposition (cf. Rev. 11:10).

---

[2] John F. Walvoord, *The Revelation of Jesus Christ* (Chicago: Moody, 1966), 28; cf. p. 175. See also Robert L. Thomas, *Evangelical Hermeneutics* (Grand Rapids: Kregel, 2002), 232-33.

The reason why this will happen during the first half of the Seventieth Week is that "in the middle of the week [the Antichrist] will bring an end to sacrifice [*zevach* = bloody sacrifices] and grain offering [*minchah* = non-bloody sacrifices] (Dan. 9:27). As J. Dwight Pentecost explains, "This expression refers to the entire Levitical system, which suggests that Israel will have restored that system in the first half of the 70th 'seven.'"[3] The Antichrist will replace the legitimate, God-honoring Jewish worship system, which only the two witnesses can inaugurate, with his own system, namely, the Abomination of Desolation (cf. Dan. 9:27b; 12:11; Matt. 24:15; 2 Thess. 2:4; Rev. 13:14-15). *But the Antichrist cannot do this until the 1,260 days of ministry allotted by God to the two witnesses have been completed* (cf. Rev. 11:7).

Third, the Lord Jesus issued this command to Jews of the Tribulation period: "When you see the 'abomination of desolation,' spoken of by Daniel the prophet, standing in the holy place ... then let those who are in Judea flee to the mountains ... For then there will be great tribulation, such as has not been since the beginning of the world until this time, no, nor ever shall be" (Matt. 24:15-16, 21). Here an obvious question arises: Would the two Jewish witnesses remain in Jerusalem during the forty-two months of Antichrist's dominion if the Lord Jesus, their Messiah, told them to flee to the mountains?

Fourth, if the 1,260 days occur during the last half of the Week, then the entire world would be celebrating the death of the two witnesses for three and a half days after the Battle of Armageddon and the destruction of the Antichrist! This is very difficult to imagine. As Gary G. Cohen explains, "At the end of the second three-and-a-half-year period, the Beast's

---

[3] J. Dwight Pentecost, "Daniel," in *The Bible Knowledge Commentary*, ed. John F. Walvoord and Roy B. Zuck (Wheaton: Victor, 1985), 1365.

followers are lamenting over Babylon and [are] gathered for the great battle of Armageddon, and [are] finally slain by Christ whose coming is surrounded with the powers of the heavens being shaken (Rev. 16–18; 19:11-21; Matt. 24:29-30). This picture does not harmonize well with the three-and-a-half days of rejoicing and gift giving in which the earth dwellers participate following the murder of the witnesses (Rev. 11:10). This discordance between the end of the second three-and-a-half-year period and the three-and-a-half days *following the end* of the three-and-a-half-year ministry of the witnesses makes it most unlikely that the prophesying of God's two servants takes place during the latter half of the week."[4]

Fifth, putting the two witnesses into the last half of the Week compromises the totality of Antichrist's dominion during that same period. How can he bring fire from heaven upon *his* enemies (through the False Prophet, Rev. 13:13) if the two witnesses are simultaneously bringing fire from heaven upon *their* enemies (Rev. 11:5)? We are clearly dealing with two different time periods: the first half of the Week with the overwhelming power of the two witnesses, and the last half of the Week with the overwhelming power of the Beast and the False Prophet. When the world asks the rhetorical question, "Who is able to make war with [the Beast]?" (Rev. 13:4), it seems obvious that no one can answer, "The two witnesses are able to make war with him," for their 1,260 days of ministry will have ended, and they will be gone.

Sixth, our Lord stated that "Elijah is coming first *and will restore all things*" (Matt. 17:11, italics added). Whoever "Elijah" turns out to be,[5] his spectacular success (under God) in bring-

---

[4] Gary G. Cohen, "The Chronology of the Book of Revelation" (Th.D. diss., Grace Theological Seminary, 1966), 251.

[5] See "The Identity of the Two Witnesses," pages 114 and following.

ing Israel back to her Messiah *must be during the first half of the Seventieth Week,* for Isaiah prophesied that Israel will have given birth "to her children" as soon as her time of tribulation begins (Isa. 66:8).

Furthermore, the basically regenerated nation, called "the woman" in Revelation 12, will flee into the wilderness and be nourished by God for 1,260 days (Rev. 12:6, 14; cf. Isa. 26:20-21), namely, the last half of the Week. "The dragon," Satan, will then "make war with the rest of her offspring, who keep the commandments of God and have the testimony of Jesus Christ" (Rev. 12:17), presumably the 144,000 witnesses from the twelve tribes of Israel and the multitudes of their Gentile converts.

The crucial question, then, is this: By whose testimony is the nation of Israel brought into the blessing of the new covenant of Jeremiah 31:31-34 (cf. Jer. 32:37-41; Ezek. 36:25-28)? And by whose witness are 12,000 from each of the twelve tribes led to the Lord, so that, as our Savior promised, "this gospel of the kingdom will be preached in all the world [during the last half of the Week] as a witness to all the nations, and then the end will come" (Matt. 24:14)?

The prophet Malachi provides the answer: "Behold, I will send you Elijah the prophet *before* the coming of the great and dreadful day of the LORD [i.e., the final 42 months of the Seventieth Week]. And he will turn the hearts of the fathers to the children, and the hearts of the children to their fathers" (Mal. 4:5-6, italics added). Our Lord, of course, was referring to this final statement of the Old Testament when He assured Peter, James, and John, "Indeed, Elijah is coming first and will restore all things" (Matt. 17:11).

Some have mistakenly assumed that Israel as a nation cannot be converted until they look upon the One "whom they pierced" (Zech. 12:10), namely, at Christ's second coming

111

in glory. But our Lord insisted: "Blessed are those who have not seen and yet have believed" (John 20:29). These words were spoken to Thomas, who refused to believe until he could "see in His hands the print of the nails" (vs. 25). Was Thomas converted when he did see the marks of his Lord's crucifixion? No, for he, like the other ten apostles, was already a born-again believer (cf. John 13:10-11). Likewise, Israel will be filled with contrition when they finally see the Savior whom they crucified, and they "will mourn for Him as one mourns for his only son," with "all the families that remain, every family by itself, and their wives by themselves" (Zech. 12:10, 14). Doubtless, this will also be the occasion when they will cry out, "Surely He has borne our griefs ... yet we esteemed Him stricken, smitten of God, and afflicted" (Isa. 53:4-5). Thus, there will be at least a forty-two-month gap between Israel's conversion and the overwhelming sight of their pierced Savior.

Immediately following the rapture of the Church, there will be no believers left on this planet. Assuming that God never leaves Himself without a witness in the world, the two witnesses will suddenly appear in Jerusalem to begin their powerful work. In the words of Alva J. McClain, founder and president of Grace Theological Seminary, "The effect of their testimony is very impressive, appearing very early in the Book of Revelation and probably accounting for the martyrs seen under the fifth seal (6:9). In chapter 7 the effect greatly expands, including the 144,000 Israelites (vss. 3-8), and also the great multitude, which no man can number, of all nations" (vss. 9-14).[6] His colleague and successor, Herman A. Hoyt, agreed: "The importance of their testimony cannot be over-

---

[6] Alva J. McClain, *The Greatness of the Kingdom* (Winona Lake, IN: BMH, 1959), 458.

estimated (Rev. 11:4) ... By their testimony, it is my opinion, they bring about the conversion of the 144,000 who will become the witnesses during the final half of the tribulation period."[7] In addition to my personal mentors, Alva J. McClain and Herman A. Hoyt, several others have concluded that the two witnesses will proclaim the gospel of the kingdom (i.e., the true gospel of the saving work of Christ as a prerequisite for entering the kingdom) during *the first half* of the Seventieth Week.[8]

---

[7] Herman A. Hoyt, *Studies in Revelation* (Winona Lake, IN: BMH, 1977), 74.

[8] Cf. James L. Boyer, "Notes on the Book of Revelation" (Christian Workman Schools of Theology), 22. (See www.whitcombministries.org for more details); Gary G. Cohen, "The Chronology of the Book of Revelation," 251-54 and Cohen's *Understanding Revelation* (Chicago: Moody, 1978), 46, 133-35; Tom Davis, *The Revelation of Jesus Christ* (Schroon Lake, NY: Word of Life Bible Institute, 2005), 30; Theodore Epp, *Practical Studies in Revelation* (Lincoln, NE: Back to the Bible, 1970), 144; Arno Froese, *119 Most Frequently Asked Questions About Prophecy* (Columbia, SC: The Olive Press, 2003), 152-53; Arnold G. Fruchtenbaum, *The Footsteps of the Messiah*, rev. ed. (Tustin, CA: Ariel Ministries, 2003), 240, 250; Robert Gromacki, *Revelation* (Schaumburg, IL: Regular Baptist Press, 2000), 65-66; I. M. Haldeman, *Synopsis of the Book of Revelation* (self-published in a pamphlet series, n.d., listed in Walvoord, *The Revelation of Jesus Christ*, 178), 13; Hippolytus, in *The Ante-Nicene Fathers* 5:248, col. B, fragment 39, 184 (documented by J. B. Smith, *A Revelation of Jesus Christ*, 170-71; see below); Thomas Ice and Timothy Demy, *Prophecy Watch* (Eugene, OR: Harvest House, 1998), 160, 164; Thomas Ice, "Why Futurism?" in *The End Times Controversy*, ed. Tim LaHaye and Thomas Ice (Eugene, OR: Harvest House, 2003), 414; Harry A. Ironside, *Revelation* (Neptune, NJ: Loizeaux, 1930), 191; Alan Johnson, "Revelation" in *The NIV Bible Commentary*, ed. Kenneth L. Barker and John Kohlenburger III (Winona Lake, IN: BMH, 1994), 1175; Tim LaHaye, "Twelve Reasons Why This Could Be the Terminal Generation," in *When the Trumpet Sounds*, ed. Thomas Ice and Timothy Demy (Eugene, OR: Harvest House, 1995), 441; David Larsen, *Jews, Gentiles, and the Church* (Grand Rapids: Discovery House, 1995), 274, 293; David M. Levy, *Revelation: Hearing the Last Word* (Bellmawr, NJ: Friends of Israel,

An interesting parallel to the amazing effects of the preaching of the two witnesses may be found in the ministry of the apostle Paul at the school of Tyrannus in Ephesus: "And this continued for two years, so that all who dwelt in Asia heard the word of the Lord Jesus, both Jews and Greeks" (Acts 19:10).

The Identity of the Two Witnesses[9]

For 2,400 years Jews have anticipated the literal return of Elijah as the forerunner of Messiah. At the Passover meal (the seder), "there is an extra place setting and a special cup on the Seder table designated just for Elijah ... The meal is followed by a prayer, and a member of the family is then asked to go to the door, open it, and see if Elijah the prophet is coming."[10] This expectation, of course, is based on the final words of the prophet Malachi at the very end of our Old Testament:

1995), chart following p. 287; Robert Lightner, *Last Days Handbook* (Nashville: Thomas Nelson, 1997), 16; William R. Newell, *The Book of Revelation* (Chicago: Moody, 1935), 158-60; Charles C. Ryrie, *Revelation* (Chicago: Moody, 1996), 84; J. B. Smith, *A Revelation of Jesus Christ* (Scottsdale, PA: Herald, 1961), 170-71; Wilbur M. Smith, "Revelation" in *Wycliffe Bible Commentary*, ed. Charles F. Pfieffer and Everett F. Harrison, (Chicago: Moody, 1962), 1510; Gerald Stanton, *Kept From the Hour* (Miami Springs, FL: Schoettle, 1992), 187-88; Lehman Strauss, *The Book of Revelation* (Neptune, NJ: Loizeaux, 1964), 218; Harold L. Wilmington, *The King Is Coming* (Wheaton, IL: Tyndale House, 1981), 166.

[9] Adapted from John C. Whitcomb, "Elijah Is Coming," *Conservative Grace Brethren Publications* (June, 1999), 24-34; used by permission. Cf. Timothy Demy and John C. Whitcomb, "Witnesses, Two," in *The Popular Encyclopedia of Bible Prophecy*, ed. Tim LaHaye and Ed Hindson, eds. (Eugene, OR: Harvest House, 2004), 401-3.

[10] Bruce Scott, *The Feasts of Israel* (Bellmawr, NJ: Friends of Israel, 1997), 44, 47, 54. Cf. Alfred Edersheim, *The Life and Times of Jesus the Messiah* (New York: Longman, Green, and Co., 1896), Vol. 1:142-43; 2:706-9.

"Behold, I will send you Elijah the prophet before the coming of the great and dreadful day of the LORD. And he will turn the hearts of the fathers to the children, and the hearts of the children to their fathers, lest I come and strike the earth with a curse" (Mal. 4:5-6).

When Peter, James, and John beheld *Elijah* on the Mount of Transfiguration, they were astounded. Could it really be true that Elijah would personally, physically, and visibly appear as the forerunner of Christ at the inauguration of His kingdom? A week before they climbed this mountain, the Lord Jesus had told them, "Assuredly, I say to you, there are some standing here who shall not taste death till they see the Son of Man coming in His kingdom" (Matt. 16:28). So this was a foretaste, a powerful visual aid, of the manner in which the Son of Man will return to the earth: personally, physically, and visibly, in glory (cf. Acts 1:11).

But why did this preview also include the visible presence of Elijah? Peter, James, and John were very concerned about this. Coming down from the mountain, they asked the Lord, "'Why then do the scribes say that Elijah must come first?' Jesus answered and said to them, 'Indeed, Elijah is coming first and will restore all things'" (Matt. 17:10-11). Thus, The Lord Jesus was agreeing with the scribes that the prophecy of Malachi should be interpreted literally, just as the chief priests and scribes had interpreted Micah 5:2 literally when they were asked concerning the birthplace of the Messiah (Matt. 2:3-6).[11]

---

[11] The ultimate tragedy, or course, was the refusal of the Jews to worship Jesus when they understood perfectly His claim to be God's Son and saw His undeniable Messianic sign-miracles (John 5:18-47). Many orthodox Jews today are still waiting for a personal Messiah; but they do not believe He will have a divine nature. Peter himself, while on the Mount, was confused as to the absolute uniqueness of the Lord Jesus in contrast to Elijah and Moses (Matt. 17:4), even though God the Father had illumined

The Greatness of John the Baptist

Now this created a great dilemma for the disciples. If Elijah was to prepare Israel for the kingdom (which they expected to happen at any moment), when and how would he appear, and how did John the Baptist, their former (and now dead) mentor (John 1:35-40) fit into the scenario? Was not the Baptizer "the burning and shining lamp," in whose "light" the disciples "were willing for a time to rejoice" because he had "borne witness to the truth" (John 5:33-35)? Was he not "more than a prophet" (Matt. 11:9)? Was he not the fulfillment of Isaiah 40:3 ("The voice of one crying in the wilderness: 'Prepare the way of the LORD,'" cf. Matt. 3:3)? Was he not the Lord's "messenger," whom God would send "to prepare the way before [Him]" (Mal. 3:1; cf. Matt. 11:10)? In fact, the Lord Jesus asserted that "among those born of women there has not risen one greater than John the Baptist" (Matt. 11:11). Thus, in the mind of our Lord, John was personally and prophetically at least as great as Enoch, Noah, Abraham, Isaac, Jacob, Joseph, Moses, Joshua, David, Solomon, Isaiah, Jeremiah, Ezekiel, Daniel – and even Elijah!

Israel's Responsibility

It is perfectly clear, then, that it was not because of some lack of dedication or wisdom that John the Baptizer failed to bring Israel to the place of spiritual readiness to acknowledge Jesus of Nazareth as the long-awaited Messiah. The national

---

him on this matter a week earlier (Matt. 16:17; cf. 2 Peter 1:16-18)! God's explanation for human suppression of biblical Christology is that "no one can say, 'Jesus is Lord' except by the Holy Spirit" (1 Cor. 12:3). For a helpful study of the deity of Messiah, see Ron Rhodes, *Christ Before the Manger: The Life and Times of the Preincarnate Christ,* (Grand Rapids: Baker, 1992). Cf. John N. Oswalt, *The Book of Isaiah: Chapters 40-66,* (Grand Rapids: Eerdmans, 1988), 328, 336.

rejection of Jesus was entirely the fault of the people and their leaders! With respect to John, therefore, our Lord explained, "If you are willing to receive it, he is Elijah who is to come" (Matt. 11:14). Then, amazingly, He added, "'Elijah has come already, and they did not know him but did to him whatever they wished'... Then the disciples understood that He spoke to them of John the Baptist" (Matt. 17:12-13).

Thus, *John could have been Elijah if Israel had accepted his message.* This is a theme that dominates the entire Bible – *men are responsible moral agents before God* and can never reject this accountability by arguing that since *God is the sovereign LORD of history* they cannot make genuine choices (cf. Rom. 9:18-24). Judas Iscariot could have reasoned: "Since my betrayal of the Messiah has been predestined [e.g., Luke 22:22a: "Truly, the Son of Man goes as it has been determined."], I have been deprived of my freedom of choice and am therefore innocent!" But our Lord, anticipating such depraved thinking, added, "But woe to that man by whom He is betrayed!" (Luke 22:22b; cf. Acts 2:23 concerning the entire nation). Thus, Joseph could say to his murderous brothers: "As for you, you meant evil against me; but God meant it for good, in order to ... save many people alive" (Gen. 50:20).

There are at least three reasons for concluding that John was *not* Elijah. First, the angel Gabriel announced to Zacharias the priest concerning his son John: "He will also go before Him *in the spirit and power of Elijah*" (Luke 1:17). Therefore, he was not literally Elijah. Second, our Lord stated, soon after the death of John, "Elijah is coming first and will restore all things" (Matt. 17:11). Thus, the Lord Jesus interpreted Malachi's prophecy literally: "Behold, I will send you Elijah the prophet" (Mal. 4:5). Third, the leaders of Israel confronted John with a direct question: "Are you Elijah?" His answer was unequivocal: "I am not" (John 1:21).

However, in spite of the fact that John was not Elijah, *his offer of the kingdom to Israel was absolutely genuine*: "Repent, for the kingdom of heaven is at hand!" he said (Matt. 3:2). This identical appeal was made by our Lord (4:17) and by the Twelve (10:7) and the Seventy (Luke 10:9-11). Therefore, no Jew could say, "We never heard a clear and genuine offer of the kingdom!"

The Theological Antinomy

But here we must face a great theological antinomy, that is, an apparent contradiction of logic that mere human intelligence cannot resolve. First, *the offer* of the kingdom was absolutely genuine. *The contingency was this: the coming of the kingdom was dependent upon the believing response of the nation of Israel.* Without national repentance on the part of God's chosen people, there can be no messianic kingdom on this earth (see Rom. 11:12, 15, 25-29, and many Old Testament prophecies). Also, for individuals, whether Jew or Gentile, there can be no salvation without genuine faith in God and His Word. This is a fundamental reality in all human history under God.

Second, at the same time, God had planned from all eternity that the kingdom offer would be rejected at Christ's first coming and would be accepted at His second coming.[12] Yes, we always need to be reminded of Deuteronomy 29:29, "The secret things belong to the LORD our God, but those things which are revealed belong to us and to our children forever," and Isaiah 55:8-9, "'For My thoughts are not your thoughts, nor are your ways My ways,' says the LORD. 'For

---

[12] Arnold G. Fruchtenbaum has pointed out, in light of Mark 9:9-13, that "if Elijah had come before the first coming of Christ and restored all things, then the prophecies of the sufferings of the first coming would remain unfulfilled" (*The Footsteps of the Messiah*, 90).

as the heavens are higher than the earth, so are My ways higher than your ways, and My thoughts than your thoughts.'"

No Jew could escape the ultimate urgency of the Baptizer's message by reasoning: "John himself admits that he is not Elijah. Therefore, since the kingdom cannot come until Elijah appears, we have no need to humble ourselves before this non-Elijah!" To excuse themselves, the Jewish leaders finally concluded that John had a demon (cf. Matt. 11:18)!

A similar dilemma faces people today. No one, however exalted (in political, social, economic, educational, or scientific realms), may dismiss the urgency of the gospel message because of the personality traits of the messenger. Like the Corinthians long ago, people in our day sometimes make a great issue of who won them to the Lord and/or baptized them. Paul's response to the Corinthians was pointed: "Who then is Paul, and who is Apollos, but ministers through whom you believed, as the Lord gave to each one" (1 Cor. 3:5; cf. 1:12-17; 3:21-23; 4:6).

John's appearance and lifestyle (like Elijah's, 2 Kings 1:8; cf. Zech. 13:4) were not impressive to sophisticated Jews: a garment of camel's hair and a diet of locusts and wild honey (Matt. 3:4). Who among the leaders would want to be identified with such a strange-looking character? But God intended for his appearance to be a rebuke to the luxurious materialism of the royal family and the Pharisees and the priests (Matt. 11:8). Many of the common people, however, did respond to his powerful preaching (Matt. 3:5-6; 11:12; 21:26).

Thus, to summarize the antinomy: God assures us, on the basis of His unchangeable foreknowledge, that Elijah – not John – will bring the nation to repentance. But human responsibility required that John's message be received with genuine repentance and faith, just as fervently as if Elijah himself had been God's messenger.

Has Elijah Been Glorified?

Elijah is coming back as a messenger to Israel. But how can he come back to the earth in a physical, mortal body? Was he not last seen being swept "to heaven" by a whirlwind (2 Kings 2:11)? This is a major reason why many evangelical theologians deny that Elijah can literally return to the earth and be killed (Rev. 11:7). If Elijah was glorified without dying, how can he return to the earth and die?

A very important factor in solving this problem may be found in our Lord's statement: "No one has ascended to heaven, but ... the Son of Man" (John 3:13). In the immediate context, our Lord was explaining to Nicodemus that He alone could testify concerning things in heaven, because He alone had been there. While this statement sheds significant light on our Lord's unique authority to speak of "heavenly things," His statement also seems to exclude the possibility that anyone, including Enoch and Elijah, could ever have ascended to the third heaven.

Furthermore, the Lord Jesus was "the firstfruits of those who have fallen asleep," in the sense of receiving a glorified body (1 Cor. 15:20); and no one else will receive such a body until "those who are Christ's" have that inconceivably marvelous experience "at His coming" (v. 23). Technically, of course, it could be argued that our Lord was referring only to a resurrection from the dead and that neither Enoch nor Elijah had died. But in light of the "firstfruits" statement of 1 Corinthians 15:20 and 23, it is very difficult to believe that two men could have been physically glorified before the Savior was glorified.

Renald E. Showers agrees that "Enoch and Elijah did not receive glorified bodies when God took them from the earth." But he also finds strong evidence in Hebrews 11:5 that Enoch did not "see," or experience, death (cf. Luke 2:26). The text states that the very purpose for God's taking Enoch was so that he should not experience death.[13] So we are left with the question of Enoch's condition after he was "taken up." A similar question may be asked concerning Korah, Dathan, and Abiram, who "went down alive into the pit [Sheol]" (Num. 16:33). My understanding would be that they *did* die after disappearing from the sight of men.

After the glorification of Christ, the apostle Paul "was caught up to the third heaven ... into Paradise" (2 Cor. 12:2, 4). But he was not glorified, for the experience was temporary, and he returned to the earth with a mortal body (complete with a sin nature) and finally died. The truly amazing statement, however, is that he didn't know whether his brief visit in heaven was "in the body or out of the body" (v. 3). Renald Showers sees 2 Corinthians 12:2-3, therefore, as indicating that Paul "believed in the possibility of a human being in a mortal body being caught up to and existing in God's heaven for some period of time."[14]

This brings us again to the fascinating statement of Hebrews 11:5: "By faith Enoch was taken away so that he did not see death." The termination of his life on earth was totally different from that of any before him – he simply disappeared! Now it should be noted that two other God-honored men in the Old Testament shared the distinction of leaving this world with no one seeing them dying or dead – *Moses* (Deut. 32:48-

---

[13] Renald E. Showers, personal correspondence with the author, Nov. 4, 1998.

[14] Ibid.

52; 34:1-6) and *Elijah* (2 Kings 2:11-14). The author of Hebrews stated, "It is appointed for men to die once" (9:27). However, the "mystery" (divine truth once hidden but now revealed) of the rapture of the body and bride of Christ without dying (1 Cor. 15:51-52; 1 Thess. 4:15-17) is the glorious exception to this "die-once" rule. But is it really legitimate to stretch this exception to include Enoch or Elijah? Old Testament saints were not members of the body and bride of Christ to whom this "blessed hope" was exclusively given (cf. Eph. 3:4-10). That Enoch entered the realm of the righteous dead[15] without dying seems to be the teaching of Hebrews 11:5. That he was physically glorified is highly unlikely.

Enoch did not "see death." But the Scriptures do *not* say this of Elijah. In fact, there seems to be some support for the concept that Elijah finally did die after he was caught up by the whirlwind. Nearly nine hundred years after that event, three of our Lord's disciples saw *Moses* (who had died 1,400 years earlier) and *Elijah* together (Matt. 17:1-8). Since Moses could not have had a glorified body (cf. 1 Cor. 15:20, 23), the implication is quite strong that Elijah did not either. Like Samuel a thousand years earlier (1 Sam. 28:15), they were temporarily "brought up" from their place of rest in the "paradise" of pre-resurrection-of-Christ history (compare Luke 23:43 with 2 Cor. 12:2-4 and Eph. 4:8-10), which our Lord also described as "Abraham's bosom" (Luke 16:22), and which was located at that time in "the heart of the earth" (Matt. 12:40; cf. 1 Peter 3:19).

Moses and Elijah appeared briefly to Peter, James, and John but had nothing to say to them. Instead, they were conversing with their Lord. As they "talked with Him" (Luke

---

[15] Our Lord described this place as "Abraham's bosom" (Luke 16:22), "Paradise" (Luke 23:43), and a special realm within sheol/hades before His resurrection (Luke 16:23).

9:30), they "spoke of His decease [Greek, *exodus;* a euphemism for His death] which He was about to accomplish at Jerusalem" (Luke 9:31). Presumably, they were concerned about the fact that not until their great King/Priest/Messiah shed His blood upon the cross could they be fully redeemed. However, in the meantime, they had been redeemed, like Abraham (Gen. 15:6), as it were, "on credit," because the blood payment of the Lamb of God for pre-Calvary believers was already accomplished in the mind of God (cf. Rom. 3:25-26; Eph. 1:3-11). If Elijah was concerned about the "decease" his Lord was soon to accomplish in Jerusalem, the implication is that he (like Moses) had not yet been physically glorified. Thus, the fact that they appeared "in glory" on the mount was merely a temporary foretaste of their ultimate glorification at the time of Christ's second coming. A significant analogy to this experience may be seen in the face of Moses, which glowed brightly after he communed with God on Mount Sinai (Exod. 34:29-35).

On the basis of these theological inferences, then, we understand that Elijah will be brought back from the dead (like Lazarus and several others) to mortal life, and to die again three and a half years later (Rev. 11:3-13). In Bible times God raised some people from the dead *after only a few hours,* and Lazarus *after four days* (when it was evident to everyone that his body was decomposing [John 11:39]). The main point at issue here, however, is that God is not limited by time or by the availability of any part of a person's physical body in order to perform the miracle of glorious resurrection, or even the miracle of resuscitation/restoration to mortal life.

We read in 1 Corinthians 15:37-38 that God gives "to each seed its own body," and "what you sow [in death and burial], you do not sow that body that shall be." This is the basic reality of all resurrections. On the human level, we might describe it this way: God knows the unique "blueprint," or "DNA information code," of every human being and is perfectly capable of giving a person a glorified body and even another mortal body (complete with the original sin nature) after thousands of years.

Elijah and Moses

Yes, Elijah is coming back to this earth again, and he will not come alone as he did at the beginning of his first ministry. Rarely does God send a servant into a significant ministry without a coworker. Robert L. Thomas has observed: "The OT required two witnesses as competent legal testimony to secure a conviction (Deut. 17:9; 19:15; Num. 35:30; cf. Heb. 10:28). Jesus also made the number two a minimum to confirm a point of discipline (Matt. 18:16) or verify truth (John 8:17). Paul too alluded to the need of a plurality of witnesses to validate a judgment (2 Cor. 13:1; 1 Tim. 5:19)."[16]

But who will be Elijah's companion witness? Many have suggested *Enoch*, but this great antediluvian saint and prophet would not be an appropriate fellow witness with Elijah in a *prophetic ministry directed exclusively to Israel*. Far more appropriate for such a unique function would be *Moses*. For future apostate Israel, after the rapture of the Church, no men in her entire history would have greater respect and appreciation than Moses and Elijah. In fact, Moses is named *80* times in the New Testament, and Elijah *29* times (compared to Abraham, 73 times, and David, 59 times)! God raised up these men *to confront Israel in times of deep apostasy.* Moses was God's great deliverer and lawgiver for Israel, of whom He said: "There has not arisen in Israel a prophet like Moses, whom the

---

[16] Robert L. Thomas, *Revelation 8-22: An Exegetical Commentary* (Chicago: Moody, 1995), 87.

LORD knew face to face, in all the signs and wonders which the LORD sent him to do in the land of Egypt ... and by all that mighty power and all the great terror which Moses performed in the sight of all Israel" (Deut. 34:10-12). By the time our Lord appeared in Israel, the Jews actually thought that *Moses* had given them the bread in the wilderness (John 6:32)!

As for *Elijah*, surely one of the greatest of the prophets, God answered his humble prayer (cf. 1 Kings 18:36-38) by sending *fire from heaven* to consume his sacrifice on Mount Carmel, and thus to defeat the 450 prophets of Baal. and finally vindicated him by means of "a chariot of fire" and "horses of fire" to escort him out of Satan's world (2 Kings 2:11).[17] When he was almost overwhelmed by the spiritual darkness of Israel under the demonic Jezebel, Elijah identified himself with Moses by fleeing to "the cave" (Hebrew, *ha-me'ārâ*) where Moses six hundred years earlier was hidden by God as His glory passed by (1 Kings 19:8-9; Exod. 33:21-23). So highly did the Jews of Jesus' day think of Elijah that when they saw Jesus' miracles, some concluded that Elijah had returned (Matt. 16:14). And when our Savior cried out from the cross, "Eli, Eli...," they believed He was calling for "Elijah" to save Him (Matt. 27:46-49; Mark 15:34-36)![18]

When the two witnesses appear in Jerusalem at the beginning of the Seventieth Week, "they immediately begin their prophetic ministry. Just prior to this (hours, days, weeks?) the

---

[17] "The mystery surrounding Moses' death (Jude 9) and the translation of Elijah offer some corroborations of these as the two witnesses" (Thomas, *Revelation 8-22*, 88.)

[18] See the high praise of Elijah, who will "restore the tribes of Jacob," in *Ecclesiasticus* (Sirach) 48:10. Cf. H. Bietenhard, "Elijah," in *Dictionary of New Testament Theology*, ed. Colin Brown (Grand Rapids: Zondervan, 1975), 1:543-45.

rapture will have removed all the believers from the earth. Therefore, there will be no one to train these two witnesses, and no time to train them. They must be men already possessing full knowledge of the Scriptures and well seasoned for such a demanding ministry. Moses was the lawgiver; Elijah was the law-enforcer. Both will be men of experience. They will be perfectly equipped for a ministry to Israel before a worldwide audience."[19]

Neither Moses nor Elijah ever entered Jerusalem, though Moses might have seen it from a distance (Deut. 34:1-3), and Elijah wrote a letter of judgment to one of the worst kings Jerusalem ever knew (2 Chron. 21:12-15). And, as we have seen, both Moses and Elijah, emerging temporarily from "paradise" to appear on the Mount of Transfiguration, were very concerned about something soon to happen in Jerusalem (cf. Luke 9:31).

The Lord Jesus said, "It cannot be that a prophet should perish outside of Jerusalem" (Luke 13:33)! In the light of this statement, it is noteworthy that these two great Israelite prophets will not only enter Jerusalem but will also experience their second and final physical death in its streets at the hands of "the beast that ascends out of the bottomless pit" at the mid-point of the Seventieth Week (Rev. 11:7-10; cf. Dan. 9:27).

One of the most convincing evidences that *Elijah* and *Moses* will be the two witnesses in Revelation 11 is the nature of the judgment-miracles these men will perform. "If anyone wants to harm them, fire proceeds from their mouth and devours their enemies. ... These have power to shut heaven, so that no rain falls in the days of their prophecy; and they have power over waters to turn them to blood, and to strike the earth with

[19] Scott M. Libby, Pastor of the Grace Brethren Church, Coventry, VT, personal communication with the author, Sept. 20, 1998.

all plagues, as often as they desire" (Rev. 11:5-6). The first two types of judgments listed were those which *Elijah* inflicted upon Israel (three and a half years of drought, 1 Kings 17:1; cf. Luke 4:25; James 5:17; and fire from heaven upon two military detachments sent by King Ahaziah to capture Elijah, 2 Kings 1:10, 12); and the second two types of judgments (blood from water and a variety of plagues) were those which *Moses* inflicted upon Egypt (Exod. 7–12).

Why are Elijah and Moses not named as the two witnesses in Revelation 11? Perhaps the Old Testament and the Gospels are so clear on this point that the Holy Spirit deemed it unnecessary to identify them by name. Would not the final words God addressed to Israel in the Old Testament have been sufficient?[20] "Remember the Law of *Moses*, My servant, which I commanded him in Horeb for all Israel with the statutes and judgments [cf. Matt. 24:20]. Behold, I will send you *Elijah* the prophet" (Mal. 4:4-5).[21]

---

[20] It must be emphasized that the book of Revelation stands solidly upon the Old Testament, like the capstone of a pyramid upon all the levels of stone beneath it. "Of the 404 verses of the Apocalypse, there are 278 which contain references to the Jewish scriptures" (Walvoord, *The Revelation of Jesus Christ*, 31, citing Swete, who cites Westcott and Hort).

[21] Among those who identify one of the witnesses as Elijah are William Barclay, *The Revelation of John*, vol. 2, rev. ed. (Philadelphia: Westminster, 1976), 70: "Much more likely the witnesses are Elijah and Moses"; James L. Boyer, *Notes on the Book of Revelation*, 21: "One would be Elijah ... the other would probably be Moses"; M. R. DeHaan, *Revelation* (Grand Rapids: Zondervan, 1946), 159: "Elijah and Moses"; H. W. Frost, *Matthew 24 and the Revelation* (New York: Oxford University Press, 1924), 144: "Moses and Elijah" (cited by Keener, *The NIV Application Commentary*, 290 [see below]); Herman A. Hoyt, *Studies in Revelation*, 75: "Without a doubt, one of these witnesses is Elijah ... Moses may be the other"; Robert Govett, *The Apocalypse* (London: C. J. Thynne, 1920), 225-50: "Elijah and Enoch" (cited by Walvoord, *The Revelation of Jesus Christ*, 179); Craig S. Keener, *The NIV Application Commentary: Revelation* (Grand Rapids: Zondervan, 2000), 290-

Conclusion

The true Church is not destined to see the Antichrist or the two witnesses in Jerusalem. Our "blessed hope" is to see Christ our Bridegroom and our Head (Titus 2:13; 2 Cor. 11:2). Nevertheless, our covenant-keeping God also has a special appointment for His chosen people Israel (Rom. 11:25-32), and that appointment includes national repentance through the prophetic ministry of Elijah (and Moses). Even before "the great and dreadful day of the LORD" (the second half of the Seventieth Week) begins (Mal. 4:5), Zion will "give birth to her children" (Isa. 66:8), and through them (presumably disciples of the two witnesses), "this gospel of the kingdom will be preached in all the world as a witness to all the nations" (Matt.

91: "Hippolytus, Tertullian, and Jerome believed Enoch and Elijah remained alive and would return as witnesses ... such a view is not impossible"; David Larsen, *Jews, Gentiles and the Church*, 293: "Probably Moses and Elijah"; Hal Lindsey, *There's a New World Coming* (Eugene, OR: Harvest House, 1984), 152: "Elijah and Moses"; John MacArthur, *Revelation 1-11* (Chicago: Moody, 1999), 300: "They may be Moses and Elijah"; Alva J. McClain, *The Greatness of the Kingdom* (Winona Lake, IN: BMH, 1959), 457: "As to their identity, one is most certainly Elijah"; Henry M. Morris, *The Revelation Record* (Wheaton, IL: Tyndale House, 1983), 194-95: "It does seem quite probable that [Enoch and Elijah] will be Christ's two witnesses"; Walter K. Price, *The Coming Antichrist* (Chicago: Moody, 1974), 194: "Moses and Elijah"; Walter Scott, *Exposition of the Revelation of Jesus Christ* (London: Pickering & Inglis, n.d.), 230: "Probably Elijah and Moses"; J. A. Seiss, *The Apocalypse* (Grand Rapids: Zondervan, n.d.), 244-54: "Elijah and Enoch" (a very detailed defense of Enoch and Elijah); J. B. Smith, *A Revelation of Jesus Christ*, 169: "Moses and Elijah"; Targum (Aramaic Translation/Interpretation of the Hebrew Bible, cited by H. Bietenhard, "Elijah," 1:544): God will "gather the diaspora through Elijah and Moses"; Merrill Tenney, *Earth's Coming King: Revelation* (Wheaton, IL: Scripture Press, 1977), 55: "Elijah and Moses"; Robert Thomas, *Revelation 8-22*, 89: "The balance of the evidence is for an expectation of the actual return of [Moses and Elijah]."

24:14). When contemplating the destiny of ethnic Israel in the light of the unbreakable Abrahamic covenant promises, we can only say with Paul, "Oh, the depth of the riches both of the wisdom and knowledge of God! How unsearchable are His judgments and His ways past finding out!" (Rom. 11:33).

8

God's New Covenant with Israel

Biblical dispensationalism is not the easiest way to understand the Bible – but it is God's way! For example, the easiest way to "understand" the book of Revelation is to spiritualize it, as literally thousands of Bible students have done for centuries. The more difficult way, and the way that guarantees God's promised blessing to the one who "reads and those who hear the words of this prophecy" (Rev. 1:3), is to recognize that Revelation is the capstone at the very top of the pyramid of written revelation and that it builds upon and presupposes the truths revealed by God in the previous sixty-five books.

Revelation 2 and 3 can be understood only in the light of the book of Acts and the Epistles, which reveal God's plan and purpose for the Church. Revelation 4–19 deals with the application of the new covenant to national Israel and her relationship to Gentile nations during the seven years that precede the second coming of Christ. Revelation 20 gives us the timing and duration of events during the kingdom that was offered to Israel by John the Baptist and the Lord Jesus in the light of numerous Old Testament promises.

Revelation 21 and 22 give us absolutely spectacular glimpses into the eternal state that follows the thousand-year kingdom of Christ upon the earth. Significantly, dispensational distinctions between the Church (21:4) and Israel (21:12-13) and the Gentiles (21:24-26) are identified and confirmed.

So here is the divine challenge for understanding such complexities as the new (Abrahamic) covenant: "Be diligent to present yourself approved to God as a workman who does not need to be ashamed, accurately handling the word of truth" (2 Tim. 2:15). Paul went on to explain that the reason the Bible (including the book of Revelation!) is "profitable for teaching" is that "all Scripture is inspired (= God-created) by God" (2 Tim. 3:16). No wonder that many Bereans "believed" and proved to be "more noble-minded than those in Thessalonica." The reason? "They received the word with great eagerness, examining the Scriptures daily, to see whether these things [that Paul taught them] were so" (Acts 17:11-12).

By way of contrast, how devastating it must have been for the two disciples on the road to Emmaus to hear the Lord say to them: "O foolish men and slow of heart to believe in all that the prophets have spoken! ... Then beginning with Moses and with all the prophets, He explained to them the things concerning Himself in all the Scriptures" (Luke 24:25-27).

Kingdom Teaching

How precious would be a tape recording of that lecture! And even more, a tape recording of the teachings our Lord gave to the disciples during His last forty days on earth, "speaking of the things concerning the kingdom of God" (Acts 1:3). He must have told them that the kingdom for which they had been praying (Matt. 6:10) was primarily a future, earthly kingdom, for they urgently asked Him, "Lord, is it at this time You are restoring the kingdom to Israel?" (Acts 1:6). It is perfectly obvious that He did not rebuke them for believing in the future establishment of a literal kingdom for Israel! He simply informed them that the timing was yet to be revealed: "It is not for you to know times or epochs which the Father has fixed by His own authority" (v. 7).

But what did our Lord tell them about the kingdom during those forty days? He must have told them that one must be "born again" to enter the kingdom, just as He had told Nicodemus (John 3:3-10). One night that Jewish theologian came to the Lord Jesus at His temporary residence in Jerusalem and told Him, "Rabbi, we know that You have come from God as a teacher; for no one can do these signs that You do unless God is with him" (John 3:2). Was our Lord thrilled to hear these words from "a ruler of the Jews," one who was, in fact, "the teacher of Israel" (3:1, 10)?

No, for Nicodemus was one of those in Jerusalem who "believed in His name" when they saw the signs He was doing (John 2:23). "But Jesus ... was not entrusting Himself to them, for He knew ... what was in man" (2:24-25). Being impressed — even astounded — by the sign-miracles of the Savior was not enough! Something deeper had to happen, as Nicodemus was about to learn (see John 6:66 and 8:31).

In one sense, Nicodemus was "not far from the kingdom." First, he, like all Jews who saw Jesus' miracles, denied that they were merely sleight-of-hand tricks! Second, he (in contrast to some leaders in Israel) rejected the idea that Jesus' works were demonic (cf. John 7:20; 8:48, 52; 10:20). Obviously, demons would not cast out demons and heal the sick (Matt. 12:22-37)! And third, he risked his reputation with the Sanhedrin by coming to Jesus personally to explain his perspectives.

"You Must Be Born Again"

Nicodemus might have expected the Lord Jesus to say: "Welcome, sir! We need someone of your reputation to join our group. So far, we have only some fishermen and a former tax collector. Thank you for coming!" Instead, he heard words he would never forget: "Truly, truly, I say to you, unless one is born again he cannot see the kingdom of God" (John 3:3). This prominent, reputable, intelligent, religious Jew needed something of infinite significance—new birth!

Nicodemus did not understand this. "How can a man be born when he is old?" he asked (John 3:4). Then came our Lord's profound reply: "Truly, truly, I say to you, unless one is born of water and the Spirit he cannot enter into the kingdom of God" (v. 5). And then came the rebuke: "Are you the teacher of Israel and do not understand these things?" (v. 10).

This is the vital question we must ask: What was Nicodemus to have understood about "new birth" (that is, regeneration) from the Old Testament? What should he have known about being "born of water and the Spirit"? The answer is really quite clear. This was nothing less than the dynamics of new covenant faith, by which Abraham had been justified before God—"He [Abraham] believed in the LORD; and He [the Lord] reckoned it to him as righteousness" (Gen. 15:6; cf. Rom. 4:3, 9, 22; Gal. 3:6; James 2:23). This was the same way every pre-Pentecost saint was saved, all the way back to Adam and Eve (Gen. 3:20-21). This is the profound—yes, *infinite*—significance of the new covenant in its spiritual aspect! Without it no one could be forgiven, saved, or born again. Without it no one could qualify for entrance into the coming kingdom or heaven!

But how could our thrice-holy God (cf. Isa. 6:3) totally justify these sinful humans of the Old Testament era on the basis of simple faith? The amazing answer is this: they were saved, as it were, "on credit." They were "justified as a gift by His grace through the redemption which is in Christ Jesus ...

133

because in the forbearance of God He passed over the sins previously committed; for the demonstration ... of His righteousness at the present time, so that He would be just and the justifier of the one who has faith" (Rom. 3:24-26; cf. Heb. 9:15). Indeed, all Old Testament believers, "having gained approval through their faith, did not receive what was promised, because God had provided something better for us, so that apart from us they would not be made perfect" (Heb. 11:39-40). Were they truly saved—born again? Yes! For "the just shall live by his faith" (Hab. 2:4; cf. Rom. 1:17; Gal. 3:11; Heb. 10:38).

In this sense, the apostle Paul insisted Abraham was "the father of all those who believe ... that righteousness might be credited" to all, both Jew and Gentile, who believe God's Word (Rom. 4:11; cf. v. 24). Nicodemus, "the teacher of Israel," should have known this!

It may be surprising to some to learn that Moses himself understood that keeping the law was not the way of salvation! He knew something profound had to happen in the hearts of people—they had to experience something supernatural, like being "born again" or "born from above." He told Israel, "[Some day] you will seek the LORD your God, and you will find Him if you search for Him with all your heart and all your soul" (Deut. 4:29). To "seek Him" means to come to Him with a humbled spirit (cf. 2 Chron. 7:14). "Yet," Moses sadly announced, "The LORD has not given you [the entire nation, with some exceptions, such as Moses himself, his brother Aaron and sister Miriam, and Joshua and Caleb] a heart to know, nor eyes to see, nor ears to hear" (Deut. 29:4). But, he added, some glorious day, "you," the entire nation, will "return to the LORD your God and obey Him with all your heart and soul" (30:2), and you (Israelites) "will love the LORD your God with all your heart and with all your soul, so that you may live" (30:6). Eight hundred years later, God confirmed this through the prophet Jeremiah: "I will put My law within them and on their heart I will write it; and I will be their God, and they shall be My people" (Jer. 31:33; cf. 32:39).

Our Lord told Nicodemus new birth meant being "born of water and the Spirit" (John 3:5). Listen to God's promise through Ezekiel: "I will take you from the nations ... and bring you into your own land. Then I will sprinkle clean water on you, and you will be clean; I will cleanse you from all your filthiness ... I will give you a new heart and put a new spirit within you; and I will remove the heart of stone from your flesh and give you a heart of flesh. I will put My Spirit within you and cause you to walk in My statutes, and you will be careful to observe My ordinances" (Ezek. 36:24-27).

What is this "clean water" that cleanses from sin? It is obviously the Word of God. Our Lord explained to His disciples, "You are already clean because of the word which I have spoken to you" (John 15:3). The apostle Paul confirmed this: "Christ also loved the church and gave Himself up for her, so that He might sanctify her, having cleansed her by the washing of water with the word" (Eph. 5:25-26). And so also did the apostle Peter, who wrote, "You have in obedience to the truth purified your souls ... for you have been born again ... through the living and enduring word of God" (1 Peter 1:22-23).

> Our Lord was astonished that Nicodemus had no understanding of these things (John 3:9-12). The Old Testament was clear about the need for a spiritual relationship with God. Mere ritual was never enough to satisfy God, as the prophets proclaimed time and time again. Surely Nicodemus, from his position as teacher in Is-

rael, should have known these things. Alas, he did not, and his spiritual blindness was typical of the vast majority in the nation who had long ago lost sight of God's spiritual dealings. The people had substituted perfunctory performance of religious ritual and observance of rabbinical traditions.[1]

The most urgent question, dear friend, is this: have we been born again through faith in Christ? Has the Spirit of God, through the Word of God—the Bible—cleansed us from the guilt of sin in the sight of our holy Creator? Remember, "He saved us, not on the basis of deeds which we have done in righteousness [e.g., church membership, water baptism, acts of kindness], but according to His mercy, by the washing of regeneration and renewing by the Holy Spirit" (Titus 3:5). Nicodemus later gave evidence of having experienced the new birth (cf. John 19:39). Today, if we believe the Lord Jesus Christ died for our sins and rose again from the dead, we too can be His people forever (Rom. 10:9)!

Circumcision

But what about circumcision? It is very difficult for most Christians to understand what this meant to Jews. It was the unique, physical identification of a male descendant of Abraham. But it had nothing to do with salvation! Abraham knew he was saved by believing God's Word long before he was circumcised—"He believed in the LORD; and He reckoned it to him as righteousness" (Gen. 15:6; cf. 17:1-14; Rom. 4:9-12). Moses also understood that the essential requirement for sal-

---

[1] Homer A. Kent Jr., *Light in the Darkness: Studies in the Gospel of John* (Winona Lake, IN: BMH Books, 2005), 58.

vation was *not physical circumcision but heart circumcision!* Thus, he could challenge the nation: "Circumcise *your heart*" (Deut. 10:16; cf. Jer. 4:4)! And he could promise (by the Holy Spirit) that some great day, "the LORD your God will circumcise *your heart and the heart of your descendants,* to love the LORD your God" (Deut. 30:6). The apostle Paul totally endorsed this point: "For he is not a Jew who is one outwardly, nor is circumcision that which is outward in the flesh. But he is a Jew who is one *inwardly*; and circumcision is that which is *of the heart, by the Spirit,* not by the letter; and his praise is not from men, but from God" (Rom. 2:28-29; cf. Phil. 3:3; Col. 2:11).

Nicodemus (and the Twelve, after the forty days) also should have known the parallel truth: Israel's greatest problem was *"their uncircumcised heart,"* which needed to be "humbled" (Lev. 26:41). Jeremiah predicted: "'Behold, the days are coming,' declares the LORD, 'that I will punish all who are circumcised [physically] and yet *uncircumcised* [spiritually] … for all the nations are uncircumcised, and all the house of Israel are *uncircumcised of heart*" (Jer. 9:25-26). When the kingdom comes, "no foreigner uncircumcised in heart and uncircumcised in flesh, of all the foreigners who are among the sons of Israel, shall enter [the Lord's] sanctuary" (Ezek. 44:9).

One of the main reasons Stephen was stoned to death was this particular denunciation of the nation of Israel: "You men who are stiff-necked and *uncircumcised in heart and ears* are always resisting the Holy Spirit; you are doing just what your fathers did" (Acts 7:51). If Stephen, a Jewish deacon in the early church (cf. Acts 6:5), understood this, surely the Jewish apostles did!

In the light of all this, one might be tempted to classify physical circumcision as an evil ceremony. No! *It was given to*

Abraham by God (cf. Gen. 17:10-27), who said, "It shall be the sign of the covenant between Me and you" (Gen. 17:11; cf. Acts 7:8); and it was *confirmed to Moses* hundreds of years later (Lev. 12:3). The Lord Jesus said, "Moses has given you circumcision (not because it is from Moses, but from the fathers)" (John 7:22). God saw to it that His Son's forerunner, John, was circumcised (Luke 1:59). He also planned that His incarnate Son would be circumcised (Luke 2:21). Paul circumcised his half-Jewish disciple Timothy (Acts 16:3) – but not his Gentile convert Titus (Gal. 2:3).

The only problem with physical circumcision, of course, was the possibility of a *misinterpretation* and *misapplication* of the sign *as a means of salvation!* In the early church, this issue had to be confronted during the Council of Jerusalem, for some heretical *Jewish* believers had told some *Gentile* believers, "Unless you are circumcised according to the custom of Moses, you cannot be saved" (Acts 15:1).

In the Church, the body and bride of Christ, there is a somewhat similar, though not identical, danger. Water baptism is a symbol of Spirit baptism, not for everyone (as circumcision was for every Israelite male), but only for true, born-again, believers. But the moment it is viewed as a necessary act for the purpose of *attaining salvation (or sanctification)*, it becomes a deadly danger! Hundreds of millions of people think they have been accepted by God because of water baptism as an infant or as an adult. How disastrous!

Partaking of the bread and the cup (the eucharist) is a blessing if understood as *a memorial* of Christ's death for us (1 Cor. 11:23-26). But the minute it is seen as having saving or sanctifying significance, a great spiritual tragedy occurs. The Catechism of the Roman Catholic Church, for example, "affirms that for believers the sacraments of the New Covenant are *necessary for salvation.*" It also states, "Through baptism we are *freed from sin* and are reborn as sons of God; we become members of Christ, are incorporated into the Church and made sharers in her mission."[2]

The most urgent question for us all is this: *Have we been born again?* Has the Spirit of God, through the Word of God—the Bible—cleansed us from the guilt of sin in the sight of our holy Creator? Remember, "He saved us, not on the basis of deeds which we have done in righteousness [e.g., church membership, water baptism, acts of kindness], but according to His mercy, *by the washing of regeneration and renewing of the Holy Spirit* (Titus 3:5). Today, if we believe the Lord Jesus Christ died for our sins and rose again from the dead, we too can be His forever (Rom. 10:9).

---

[2] See note 8 in chapter 2.

PART 3

THE MILLENNIUM AND BEYOND

9

The Church and the Coming Kingdom

When the Lord Jesus Christ commanded His disciples to pray, "Thy kingdom come. Thy will be done in earth, as it is in heaven" (Matt. 6:10 KJV), they understood basically what kind of kingdom He was referring to. It was not the Church, for that body of believers, composed of Jews and Gentiles together without distinction, was explained for the first time through Paul and the other apostles after the Day of Pentecost (e.g., Eph. 3:1-10). Instead, it was the kingdom prophesied throughout the centuries of Old Testament history.

This rather obvious fact has been very difficult for the average Christian to believe. We have been told so often that the Church *is* the kingdom that we easily assume that the Church has replaced Israel forever as God's people. I am deeply grateful to God that this is not true, for if He can break His unconditional covenant promises to utterly unworthy Israel (cf. Gen. 22:15-18), then He can break His unconditional promises to the utterly unworthy Church (cf. Phil. 1:6)! We praise Him now, and shall praise Him forever, because "the gifts and calling of God are irrevocable" (Rom. 11:29).

In one sense, believers today are already, *judicially (de jure)*, in Christ's kingdom (cf. Col. 1:13), just as we are already seated with Him "in the heavenly places" (Eph. 2:6), or "in the heavenlies." But *actually (de facto)*, we still await the day when

He and His kingdom will appear on the earth. In other words, the kingdom is not yet here; it is still future.

Though the Church has been "grafted in" to God's program at the present time (Rom. 11:16-18), ethnic Israel will be reinstated into God's program in the future. The kingdom has not yet arrived. The Lord Jesus Christ is now at the right hand of the Father, but He is not yet seated upon the throne of David in Jerusalem (Ps. 110:1; Luke 1:32; Heb. 10:12-13). When His glorious kingdom finally comes to the earth, in answer to the prayers of His people, then not only redeemed and glorified Israelites but also the glorified Church under Christ, her Head and Bridegroom, will have significant functions to perform.

For one thousand years, the Church – with *glorified* Old Testament saints and Israelite martyrs of the Beast – will reign with Him over the earth (Rev. 20:4). Even the theologically and spiritually weak Corinthian church will exercise that function in the Millennium, for Paul told them: "Do you not know that the saints will judge the world? If the world is judged by you, are you not competent to constitute the smallest law courts?" (1 Cor. 6:2). Doubtless their regal and judicial position will be relatively low, for the judgment seat of Christ will bring to light all the hidden things of darkness and will determine the level of honor and privilege each saint will occupy during the kingdom (1 Cor. 3:11-15; 4:5). *Their eschatological ignorance was so profound that they actually viewed themselves – as opposed to the true apostles – to be above reproach in their regal lordship!* Paul, with a touch of irony, told them, "You have become kings without us; and indeed, I wish that you had become kings so that we also might reign with you" (1 Cor. 4:8)!

Yes, unbelievable though it may seem, all born-again Christians (men, women, and children) will function as *kings* under Christ during the coming kingdom age. Some have insisted that "unworthy" believers will be excluded from the wedding banquet and the millennial kingship and will experience a temporary "weeping and gnashing of teeth" following the judgment seat of Christ at the beginning of the Millennium. But if this is true, then the body of Christ, the true Church, will be drastically divided. Such a view reminds one of the "partial rapture" concept, whereby only "worthy" Christians are raptured before the Tribulation. But who among us is truly "worthy" of redemption, rapture, glorification, and reigning with Christ in the coming kingdom? If worthiness is the qualification, then there will be no rapture at all, nor will any Christian ever reign with Him.

Today, angels (both righteous and wicked) exercise enormous governmental powers over the world of mankind, under God (cf. Dan. 10; 1 John 5:19). But in the kingdom age, Satan and demons will have no access to man (except for "a short time" at the end of the Millennium, Rev. 20:3). Righteous angels presumably will enter into a well-deserved "retirement program" for those thousand years, for "He did not subject to angels the world to come," but rather He subjects it to human beings (Heb. 2:5-8)!

Not only will we be "kings," but we will also serve as "priests of God and of Christ" (Rev. 20:6). We will never be Levitical/Aaronic/Zadokian priests, for they will

- be physical descendants of Zadok, David's faithful high priest;
- escape martyrdom during the Seventieth Week; and thus
- be available to serve nonglorified Israelites and Gentiles (Ezek. 44:15-31).

145

The prophet Jeremiah (of the non-Zadokian line of Abiathar priests in Anathoth) wrote, "The Levitical priests shall never lack a man before Me to offer burnt offerings, … and to prepare sacrifices continually" (Jer. 33:18). Significantly, God will identify, save, and seal 12,000 Levites by the middle of the Seventieth Week (Rev. 7:7), even though Jews today have long lost their tribal identities (since AD 70).

In all the intricate descriptions of Zadokian priestly functions in the millennial temple in Ezekiel 43–46, there is not one word about a high priest! Ezekiel must have been fully aware of the prophecy of Psalm 110:4, that Messiah would be a Melchizedekian high priest; and Zechariah must have known this too (cf. Zech. 6:13). Under this absolutely unique High Priest, we will doubtless intercede for nonglorified saints on the earth, even as Levitical priests interceded for Israelites in the pre-Pentecost era. This is a deep mystery and a marvel![1]

The precise function of the Church during the kingdom age is not revealed to us. We do know, however, that we will participate in the great inaugural banquet (Matt. 8:11; 26:29; Luke 13:28; 22:16, 18). How amazed the survivors of the Tribulation will be to behold Christ's glorious bride, the Church! Beyond that, it seems reasonable to envision our Lord appearing in Jerusalem at least at the annual Feast of Tabernacles (Ezek. 45:25; Zech. 14:16), which always anticipated God's dwelling with His people. And surely the bride will be with Him, for He promised us that "where I am, there you may be also" (John 14:3). All we can say, in the light of such kingdom promises, is, "Amen. Come, Lord Jesus" (Rev. 22:20)!

---

[1] For the distinctives of millennial worship, see the section "Israelite Worship Under the Old and New Covenants Contrasted" in chapter 11.

10

God's People and the Future of Egypt

I will not soon forget that hot Egyptian afternoon, August 5, 1952, when I climbed 450 feet to the top of the Great Pyramid of Cheops at Giza. How did this wonder of the ancient world get here?

Two and a half millennia before Christ, tens of thousands of workers spent more than 20 years gathering 2.3 million blocks of stone—some weighing up to 15 tons—on a base covering 13.1 acres to prepare an eternal home for their Pharaoh-god.

What brilliance this took! What dedication! Remember, this was not long after the dispersion of mankind from the Tower of Babel, when the Egyptians demonstrated their amazing building skills along the Nile River.

Intertwined with Israel

Two hundred years after Abraham visited Egypt (Gen. 12:10-20), Jacob and his sons—especially Joseph—must have marveled at the things they saw there (c. 1875 BC; Genesis 36–50). But the day came (in 1445 BC) when Egypt was in shambles because of her enslavement and mistreatment of God's people Israel (Exodus 7–11).

Even though "Solomon made a treaty with Pharaoh king of Egypt, and married Pharaoh's daughter" (1 Kings 3:1),[1] Egypt remained a threat to the people of Israel through the centuries. The great prophet Isaiah cried out, "Woe to those who go down to Egypt for help, and rely on horses, who trust in chariots because they are many, and in horsemen because they are very strong, but who do not look to the Holy One of Israel, nor seek the Lord!" (Isa. 31:1).

The author at the Great Pyramid, 1952.

Destined for Destruction

At the time of this writing, the land of Egypt is in turmoil. The people of Israel are afraid that radical forces will take control of Egypt and attack them. This could happen at any time; but the book of Daniel actually tells us of a final attack that will occur during the Great Tribulation—which is the next significant period of Bible prophecy.

---

[1] Scripture quotations in this chapter are from the NKJV.

About three years after the true Church has been removed from the earth, "at the time of the end the king of the South [Egypt] shall attack him [the Antichrist in Jerusalem]" (Dan. 11:40). However, at the same time, the King of the North (perhaps Russia) will attack the Antichrist, kill him (Dan. 11:40-41; cf. Rev. 13:14), and then move south.[2] "He [the King of the North] shall stretch out his hand against the countries, and the land of Egypt shall not escape. He shall have power over the treasures of gold and silver, and over all the precious things of Egypt" (Dan. 11:42-43).

Forty-two months later, Jesus Christ, the King of Kings, will descend from heaven and take over all the kingdoms of the world—including Egypt (Rev. 19:11-21). Ezekiel prophesied, "I will make the land of Egypt desolate in the midst of the countries that are desolate; and ... her cities shall be desolate forty years; and I will scatter the Egyptians among the nations and disperse them throughout the countries. Yet, thus says the Lord God: At the end of forty years I will gather the Egyptians from the peoples among whom they were scattered ... to the land of their origin, and there they shall be a lowly kingdom" (Ezek. 29:12-14).

Spiritual Transformation Awaits

Finally, when the kingdom of Christ is established upon the earth, the people of Egypt will join the peoples of all the nations to worship the God of Israel.

> In that day there will be an altar to the Lord in the midst of the land of Egypt, and a pillar to the Lord at its border. And it will be for a sign and for a witness to the Lord of hosts in the land of Egypt; ... and He will send them a Savior and a

---

[2] See chapter 6 for full discussion of these kings.

Mighty One, and He will deliver them. Then the Lord will be known to Egypt, and the Egyptians will know the Lord in that day, and will make sacrifice and offering; yes, they will make a vow to the Lord and perform it. ... In that day ... the Lord of hosts shall bless, saying, Blessed is Egypt My people ... and Israel My inheritance. (Isa. 19:19-25; cf. Gen. 15:18; Zech. 14:18-19)

How amazing are the judgments and mercies of God! In spite of all that Egypt has done and will do to hurt Israel, and in spite of all that Israel had done and will do to hurt their Lord, He remains faithful to His promises and true to His Word.

Especially—and urgently—essential for both Israel and Egypt in the meantime today is this word from heaven: "God so loved the world that He gave His only begotten Son, that whoever believes in Him should not perish but have everlasting life" (John 3:16).

A view of the lower pyramid showing parts of the original surface still in place (viewed from the top of the Great Pyramid, with my camel driver in the foreground).

11

The Millennial
Temple of Ezekiel 40 – 48

Those who have discovered that the key to interpreting God's Word properly is to understand it in a normal, literal way will also discover that Ezekiel 40–48 is not a burden to the Bible student but a delight. What a joy God brings to the heart of the believer when he realizes, perhaps for the first time, that God did not give us any portion of His Word to confuse us but rather to enlighten us. God really does mean what He says!

The last nine chapters of Ezekiel serve almost as a test case for God's people. In the words of Charles Lee Feinberg, a great Old Testament scholar of the last century,

> Along with certain other key passages of the Old Testament, like Isaiah 7:14 and 52:13–53:12 and portions of Daniel, the concluding chapters of Ezekiel form a kind of continental divide in the area of biblical interpretation. It is one of the areas where the literal interpretation of the Bible and the spiritualizing or allegorizing method diverge widely. Here amillennialists and premillennialists are poles apart. When thirty-nine chapters of Ezekiel can be treated detailedly and

seriously as well as literally, there is no valid
reason a priori for treating this large division of
the book in an entirely different manner.[1]

God will fulfill His covenant promises to Abraham, Isaac,
and Jacob. God's "chosen people" will enjoy their "promised
land" some day, after they have experienced national regeneration (Jer. 31:31-34; Rom. 11:25-26). Not just for the Church,
but also for Israel, "the gifts and the calling of God are irrevocable" (Rom. 11:29).

We now present seven arguments in support of and three
arguments in opposition to a literal interpretation of Ezekiel
40–48.

Arguments in Support of a Literal Interpretation

1. A careful reading of Ezekiel 40–42 gives one the clear
impression of a future, literal temple for Israel because of the
immense number of details concerning its dimensions, its
parts, and its contents.[2] Surely, if so much space in the Holy
Scriptures is given to a detailed description of this temple, we
are safe in assuming that it will be as literal as the tabernacle
and the temple of Solomon. The fact that its structure and
ceremonies will have a definite symbolical and spiritual significance cannot be used as an argument against its literal
existence, for the tabernacle was a literal structure in spite of
the fact that it was filled with symbolic and typical significance. Such reasoning might easily deny the literality of

---

[1] Charles Lee Feinberg, *The Prophecy of Ezekiel* (Chicago: Moody, 1967), 233.
See also John W. Schmitt and J. Carl Laney, *Messiah's Coming Temple*
(Grand Rapids: Kregel, 1997).

[2] See Erich Sauer, *From Eternity To Eternity* (Grand Rapids: Eerdmans,
1954), chapter 34; and Thomas Ice and Randall Price, *Ready to Rebuild*
(Eugene, OR: Harvest House, 1992).

Christ's glorious second coming on the basis that the passages that describe His coming are filled with symbolical expressions (see Matt. 24 and Rev. 19).

2. Ezekiel was given specific instructions to "declare to the house of Israel all that you see" (40:4), which seems strange if the temple were to symbolize only general truths. Even more significant is the fact that the Israelites were to "observe its whole design and all its statutes and do them" (43:11). This is an exact parallel to the pattern of the tabernacle, which Moses saw in the Mount and which God commanded him to construct (Exod. 25:8-9).

3. All will agree that the temple of Ezekiel 8-11 was the literal temple of Ezekiel's day, even though the prophet saw it "in the visions of God" (8:3) while he himself was still in Babylon (8:1). In these four chapters, we find mention of "the entrance of the north gate of the inner court" (8:3), "the porch" (8:16), "the altar" (8:16), "the threshold of the temple" (9:3), and "the east gate of the Lord's house" (10:19). Now without any indication whatever that an ideal temple instead of a literal temple is being set forth in chapters 40–42, we find similar, if not identical, descriptive formulas being used: "in the visions of God" (40:2; cf. 8:3), "a gateway on the inner court" (40:27 NKJV; cf. 8:3), "the porch of the temple" (40:48; cf. 8:16), "the altar" (43:18; cf. 8:16), and "the gate facing toward the east" (43:1; cf. 10:19), through which the glory of the God of Israel is seen returning, exactly as He had departed, according to 10:19 and 11:23. Now if the millennial temple is not to be a reality, then why insist that the return of the God of Israel is to be a reality?

4. Ezekiel is not the only Old Testament prophet who saw a future, glorious temple for God's chosen people Israel, complete with animal sacrifices, in the Holy Land. Note the following.

Prophecies of a millennial temple
- Joel 3:18
- Isaiah 2:3
- Isaiah 60:13
- Daniel 9:24
- Haggai 2:7, 9

Prophecies of animal sacrifices in the future temple
- Isaiah 56:6-7
- Isaiah 60:7
- Jeremiah 33:18
- Zechariah 14:16-21

5. God has definitely promised to the line of Zadok an everlasting priesthood (1 Sam. 2:35; 1 Kings 2:27, 35). This confirms God's promise of an everlasting priesthood to Zadok's ancestor, Phinehas (Num. 25:13), which also confirms His promise of an everlasting priesthood to Phinehas's grandfather, Aaron (Exod. 29:9; 40:15). See 1 Chronicles 6:1-30 for the full genealogy. Furthermore, this promise of an everlasting priesthood was strongly confirmed by God through Jeremiah, who links the perpetuity of the Levitical priests with the perpetuity of the Davidic kingship and the perpetuity of the earth's rotation on its axis (Jer. 33:17-22)! In view of these promises of God, confirmed again and again, it is highly significant that the millennial temple of Ezekiel will have the sons of Zadok as its priests (Ezek. 40:46; 44:15)! God apparently means what He says! The intrinsic probability of this being fulfilled literally is strengthened tremendously by the mention of 12,000 Levites who will be sealed by God during the yet future Seventieth Week of Daniel (Rev. 7:7). If these are literal Levites, it would hardly be consistent to maintain that the temple is spiritual or figurative. And if God's promises to Aaron, Phinehas, and Zadok are spiritualized, how can we in-

sist that His promises to David will be fulfilled literally (2 Sam. 7:13, 16)?

6. The Bible clearly teaches that while there is no such thing as an earthly temple, an altar, or animal sacrifices in true Christianity (John 4:21; Heb. 7–10), there will be such provisions for Israel following the rapture of the Church (Matt. 24:15; 2 Thess. 2:4; Rev. 11:1-2; compare also Hos. 3:4-5 with Dan. 9:24, 27). Furthermore, Revelation 20:9 indicates that Jerusalem, the "beloved city," will once again be "the camp of the saints" during the millennial age. The clear New Testament teaching of a post-rapture "holy place" and "temple of God" in Jerusalem, complete with "the altar" (Rev. 11:1), prepares us to anticipate a millennial temple in connection with the "holy city" Jerusalem, in harmony with Old Testament teaching.

7. The only real alternatives to the literal interpretation are unbelieving modernism, which does not hesitate to say that this temple was a mere figment of Ezekiel's imagination, and a fanciful idealism, usually amillennial, which says that this temple depicts certain realities of the Church that shall be fulfilled in our times or in the eternal state.[3] Andrew W. Blackwood Jr. believes that the centrality of the altar in Ezekiel's temple points to the centrality of the Communion table in the Christian Church! In light of this, Dr. Blackwood is disturbed that "in many of the beautiful Protestant churches that are being built today, the table of Holy Communion is crowded back against the wall at the greatest possible distance from the congregation, as was the medieval Roman Catholic custom. But today in the beautiful new Roman Catholic churches that

---

[3] See, for example, G. R. Beasley-Murray, "Ezekiel," in *New Bible Commentary*, revised, ed. Donald Guthrie and J. A. Motyer (Grand Rapids: Eerdmans, 1970), 684.

are being constructed the sacramental table is brought away from the wall; so that the congregation, insofar as it is physically possible, surrounds the table. Ezekiel certainly is telling us that church architecture should be an expression of theology."[4]

So widespread is this type of interpretation that even some prominent dispensationalists have been influenced by it. Dr. J. Sidlow Baxter, for example, tells us that "the main meanings of the striking symbols are clear. ... The various cube measurements symbolize their divine perfection. In the description of the sacrificial ritual we see the absolute purity of the final worship"[5] We shall leave it to the reader to decide, after studying Ezekiel 40–42 again, whether these are "clear" meanings of these "symbols." We are also very disappointed to see that even Dr. Harry Ironside, whose prophetic insight was usually very clear, fell into the same spiritualizing tendency. Notice how he attempted to spiritualize the temple river of Ezekiel 47.

> Ezekiel's guide measured a thousand cubits, that is, fifteen hundred feet, and he caused the prophet to enter into the waters: they were up to his ankles. May this not suggest the very beginning of a life of fellowship with God? 'If we live in the Spirit let us also walk in the Spirit' (Gal. 5:25). The feet were in the river and the waters covered them, but the guide measured another thousand cubits and caused Ezekiel to pass through the waters, and they were up to his knees. Who will think it fanciful if we say that the waters up to

[4] Andrew W. Blackwood, *Ezekiel: Prophecy of Hope* (Grand Rapids: Baker, 1965), 240.

[5] J. Sidlow Baxter, *Explore the Book* (Grand Rapids: Zondervan, 1960), 4:34.

the knees suggest praying in the Holy Spirit? But the guide measured another thousand and caused the prophet to pass through the waters, and now they were up to his loins, suggesting the complete control of every fleshly lust in the power of the Spirit of God. He measured another thousand, and that which had begun as a small stream was a river so that Ezekiel could not pass through, for the waters were risen, waters to swim in. Surely this is to live in the fullness of the Spirit to which every child of God should aspire.[6]

In my opinion, such an exposition of Holy Scripture is not only fanciful but also dangerous, causing the student to wonder whether each expositor is not, after all, a guide unto himself, the blind leading the blind. If the commentator rejects the literal interpretation of the passage and fails to find support elsewhere in Scripture for a consistent figurative or symbolic interpretation, he should confess his ignorance, leave the passage alone, and go elsewhere. For many centuries the Church has been subjected to various spiritualizing interpretations of Old and New Testament prophecies concerning the second coming of Christ. It is our prayer that God will raise up many faithful students of His Word in these last days who will search the prophetic Scriptures in the belief that God actually means what He says.

---

[6] Harry A. Ironside, *Expository Notes on Ezekiel the Prophet* (Neptune, NJ: Loizeaux, 1974) 327, 328.

Objections to a Literal Interpretation of Ezekiel 40–48

1. The measurements and location given for Ezekiel's temple rule out a literal understanding of it.

> The area of the temple courts (500 x 500 'reeds,' or about one square mile) would be larger than the entire ancient walled city of Jerusalem, and the holy portion for priests and Levites (20,000 x 25,000 reeds, or about 40 x 50 miles) would cover an area six times the size of greater London today and could not possibly be placed within present-day Palestine, that is between the Jordan River and the Mediterranean Sea (Ezek. 47:18), to say nothing of the 'portion of the prince' on either side of this area (45:7, 47:21). The Millennial Jerusalem would be about 40 miles in circumference and thus ten times the circumference of the ancient city. Furthermore, it would be somewhat north of the present site of the city, and the Temple area would be about ten miles north of that, on the way to Samaria! This is quite unthinkable, for such a city would not be the Jerusalem of Jewish memories and associations, and a Temple in any other locality than Mount Moriah would hardly be the Temple of Jewish hope.[7]

ANSWER: Israel will have the only sanctuary and priesthood in the world during the millennial age, so the temple courts and sacred area will need to be greatly enlarged to

---

[7] Baxter, *Explore the Book,* 4:32.

accommodate the vast number of worshippers and the priests who will serve them (Isa. 2:3; 60:14; 61:6; Zech. 8:20-23). Various Old Testament prophecies speak of great geological changes that will occur in Palestine at the time of Christ's second coming, so it is not impossible to imagine a 2,500-square-mile area for the temple and city fitted into a reshaped and enlarged land. See Isaiah 26:15; 33:17; 54:2; and especially Zechariah 14:4-10. The latter passage tells us of new valleys and rivers, and a flattening of portions of land "into a plain," which then "will rise and remain on its site." Presumably, the entire Dead Sea region will be lifted more than 1,300 feet, above the present sea level, for it will contain fish "according to their kinds, like the fish of the Great Sea, very many" (Ezek. 47:10). Revelation 16:20 informs us that at the end of the Great Tribulation gigantic earthquakes will cause islands and mountains to vanish. Thus, both Testaments speak of topographical and geographical changes that will accompany the inauguration of the millennial kingdom. Jerusalem itself will be the capital of the world, the beloved city (Rev. 20:9), and its size will surely be proportionate to its importance. If Nineveh, the capital of one ancient empire, was sixty miles in circumference (Jonah 3:3), why would it be impossible for the millennial Jerusalem to be forty?[8]

With regard to the problem of the millennial temple being located about ten miles north of Jerusalem, God specifically indicates to Ezekiel that the temple area will no longer adjoin the royal palace as in the days of old (Ezek. 43:7-9). The point is clearly stated in 43:12: "This is the law of the house: its entire area on the top of the mountain all around shall be most holy. Behold, this is the law of the house." Vast topographical changes will not make Palestine less the Promised Land for

---

[8] Ibid., 4:170.

Israel, nor will a centralized, enlarged temple ten miles removed from the city be a disappointment to Israelites who have been accustomed to thinking of it in terms of Mount Moriah. The important thing is that the glory of Jehovah will fill the temple (43:5), and the city will be renamed on the basis that "The LORD is there" (48:35).

2. It is unthinkable that a system of animal sacrifices will be reinstituted after the one perfect sacrifice of Christ has been accomplished, especially in the light of Hebrews 7–10.

ANSWER: While this might seem to be a most formidable objection to the literality of the millennial temple, several important considerations tend to modify the force of this objection.

[1] The millennial system of sacrifices described by Ezekiel differs profoundly from the Aaronic system, so that it is not simply a reinstitution of Mosaic Judaism as many have claimed. These changes could not have escaped the notice of post-captivity Jews, such as Zerubbabel and Joshua, who, seeing the glorious context into which Ezekiel placed these new ordinances, would have realized immediately that the prophecy could be fulfilled only in the kingdom age. Therefore, they made no effort to build such a temple after the exile. Dwight Pentecost points out that there will be no ark of the covenant, table of the Law, cherubim, mercy seat, veil, golden candlestick, or table of showbread. Instead of a high priest, there will be a prince who has some royal and priestly powers but will actually be neither king nor high priest. The Levites will have fewer temple privileges except for the sons of Zadok, who will serve as priests. The Feast of Pentecost is omitted, as well as the great Day of Atonement, and there is no evening sacrifice. The dimensions of the temple and courts

are changed, and they are removed from the city.[9] With regard to additions that will be made, Nathanael West states, "The entrance of the 'Glory' into Ezekiel's Temple to dwell there, forever; the Living Waters that flow, enlarging from beneath the Altar; the suburbs, the wonderful trees of healing, the new distribution of the land according to the 12 tribes, their equal portion therein, the readjustment of the tribes themselves, the Prince's portion, and the City's new name, 'Jehovah-Shammah,' all go to prove that New Israel restored is a converted people, worshipping God 'in Spirit and in Truth.'"[10]

The later rabbis, who lost the true significance of Old Testament prophecy, were deeply troubled by the contradictions between Moses and Ezekiel and hoped that Elijah would explain away the difficulties when he returns to the earth! Blackwood cites another rabbinic source to the effect that "the entire prophecy would have been excluded from the canon were it not for the devoted labor of Rabbi Hanina ben Hezekiah, a scholar of the first century A.D., who must have written an extensive commentary on Ezekiel: 'Three hundred barrels of oil were provided for him for light and he sat in an upper chamber where he reconciled all discrepancies' (*Babylonian Talmud*, Menahoth 45a)."[11] A similar dilemma confronts modern Christian scholars who deny a literal millennium. For example, the contributor to Ellicott's *Commentary on Ezekiel* twice insists that the prophecy cannot be literally fulfilled

---

[9] J. Dwight Pentecost, *Things to Come* (Grand Rapids: Zondervan, 1958), 520-24.

[10] Quoted by Pentecost, *Things to Come*, 522, citing West's, *The Thousand Years in Both Testaments*, 429.

[11] Blackwood, *Ezekiel: Prophecy of Hope*, 22.

"except on the supposition of physical changes in the land";[12] but this is exactly what the Bible tells us will happen at the time of the inauguration of the millennium. Such objections, therefore, simply beg the question.

[2] Just because animal sacrifices and priests have no place in Christianity does not mean they will have no place in Israel after the rapture of the Church; for there is a clear distinction made throughout the Scriptures between Israel and the Church.[13] And just because God will have finished His work of sanctification in the Church by the time of the rapture is no warrant for assuming that He will have finished His work of instruction, testing, and sanctification of Israel. In fact, one of the main purposes of the thousand-year earthly kingdom of Christ will be to vindicate His chosen people Israel before the eyes of all nations (Isa. 60, 61). It is obvious that the book of Hebrews was written to Christians, and we have no right to insist that Israelites during the millennium will also be Christians – without priests, without sacrifices, and without a temple. Saints like John the Baptist who died before Pentecost were not Christians (John 3:29; Matt. 11:11); and those who are saved following the rapture of the Church will likewise be excluded from membership in the bride of Christ, though they will be "made perfect" like all the redeemed (Heb. 12:23).

[3] Even in the age of grace, God deems it necessary for Christians to be reminded of the awful price that Jesus paid, through the symbolism of the bread and the cup. Drinking of this "cup of blessing" (1 Cor. 10:16) does not involve a re-offering of the blood of Christ in contradiction to the book of Hebrews, but serves as a powerful "remembrance" of Christ

---

[12] Frederic Gardiner, "Ezekiel," in *An Old Testament Commentary for English Readers,* ed. Charles John Ellicott (London: Cassell and Co., 1884), 5:315.

[13] See chapter 3, "The Church Is Not Israel."

and a powerful proclaiming of "the Lord's death until He comes" (1 Cor. 11:25-26). Likewise, in the context of distinctive Israelite worship, the five different offerings, four of them involving the shedding of blood, will serve as a constant reminder to millennial Jews (who will not yet be glorified) of the awful and complete sacrifice that their Messiah, now present in their midst, had suffered centuries before to make their salvation possible. In view of the fact that there may be no other bloodshed in the entire world because of a return of semi-Edenic conditions (cf. Isa. 11:6-9), such sacrifices upon the temple altar would be doubly impressive.[14]

However, such sacrifices will not be totally voluntary and purely memorial as is true of the Christian Eucharist. Ezekiel says that God will "accept" people on the basis of animal sacrifices (43:27), and they are "to make atonement for the house of Israel" (45:17; cf. v. 15). In other words, just as in Old Testament times, the privilege of life and physical blessing in the theocratic kingdom will be contingent upon outward conformity to the ceremonial law. Such conformity did not bring salvation in Old Testament times, but saved Israelites willingly conformed. Only faith in God could bring salvation, and this has been God's plan in every dispensation. It is a serious mistake, therefore, to insist that these sacrifices will be expiatory. They were certainly not expiatory in the Mosaic economy ("it is impossible for the blood of bulls and goats to take away sins," Heb. 10:4), and they will not be so in the millennium. But their symbolic and pedagogic value, unlike the Communion service, will be upheld by a legalistic system of enforced participation. For example, those who decide to neglect the annual Feast of Tabernacles will be punished by a

---

[14] See chapter 12 for further discussion of animal sacrifices in the millennial temple.

drought or a plague (Zech. 14:16-19). If the true significance of the five offerings be understood, it is not difficult to see how they could serve as effective vehicles of divine instruction and discipline for Israel and the nations during the kingdom age.[15]

3. When we read in Ezekiel 47:1-12 of a stream that issues from the temple and increases to a great river within a few miles with no tributaries, enters into the Dead Sea and heals it of its death, and has trees growing on its banks that have perennial foliage and fruit, the leaves being for "medicine" and the fruit, although for food, never wasting, surely we are in the realm of idealism! We find such a stream pictured in the eternal state (Rev. 22:1-2), but surely we cannot picture such a stream during the millennial age.

ANSWER: Such an objection is based largely upon the fallacious notion that the supernatural aspects of eschatology (including the descriptions of the New Jerusalem in Revelation 21 and 22) are purely idealistic pictures. Doubtless many Jews who studied the Old Testament messianic prophecies before the first coming of Christ felt the same way. But when Christ came, He changed water to wine, multiplied loaves and fish, instantly calmed a great storm, healed the sick, and raised the dead (Isa. 35:5-6; Matt. 11:5). He said that those who did not believe all that the prophets spoke were fools and "slow of heart" (Luke 24:25). In the light of these first-coming fulfillments and our Lord's strong admonition, it would seem to be the better part of wisdom to take these millennial prophecies literally. Who are we to say that there cannot be any supernatural aspects to the millennial reign of the glorified Christ on the earth? Some who deny the literality

---

[15] For a detailed discussion of the theological and exegetical issues involved, see chapter 12.

of the temple stream admit that Edenic conditions will largely prevail in that age, with longevity, universal peace, transformation of animal life, and blossoming of deserts. But if we consider carefully some of the conditions that existed in the Garden of Eden, we will discover that among them were trees and fruits that had super-vegetative powers and a stream from the garden that divided into four rivers (Gen. 2:10-14). Few who deny the literality of the temple stream of Ezekiel 47 would go so far as to deny the literality of the rivers and trees of Genesis 2. But is not this an inconsistency? Cannot God accomplish these things for His own purposes in ways we cannot now understand? If the natural processes of our present world serve as the ultimate guide for what can or cannot happen in the age to come, we not only wipe out much of biblical eschatology but also end up denying even the miraculous works of Christ. This is simply too great a price to pay to maintain the idealistic view of Ezekiel's prophecies.[16]

---

[16] For a helpful analysis of the millennial temple prophecy of Ezekiel 40-48, see Charles Lee Feinberg, *The Prophecy of Ezekiel: The Glory of the Lord* (Chicago: Moody, 1969), 233-79. See also Arnold G. Fruchtenbaum, "The Millennial Religion," in *One World*, ed. Ron J. Bigalke, Jr. (Springfield, MO: 21st Century Press, 2005), 431-456.

12

Christ's Atonement and Animal Sacrifices in Israel[1]

The future function of the millennial temple (Ezekiel 40–48) has long been problematic for dispensationalists in view of the finished work of Christ. Light is shed on this problem by noting the original theocratic purpose of Old Testament

[1] The author expresses his appreciation to John A. Sproule, former professsor of New Testament and Greek, Grace Theological Seminary, for his careful interaction with this study, especially from the perspective of the book of Hebrews; and to Richard E. Averbeck, former professor of Old Testament and Hebrew, for his keen insights on Old Testament covenants and the function of "atonement" in Leviticus and Ezekiel. Research papers by the following graduate students at Grace Theological Seminary have also been of considerable assistance: David R. Webb (1980), Robert L. Maziasz (1980), and David C. Wagner (1985). More recently, Jerry M. Hullinger has written an outstanding Th.D. dissertation, "A Proposed Solution to the Problem of Animal Sacrifices in Ezekiel 40-48" (Dallas Theological Seminary, 1993). See also his articles, "The Problem of Animal Sacrifices in Ezekiel 40-48" in *Bibliotheca Sacra* 152 (July-Sept. 1995), 279-89; "The Divine Presence, Uncleanness, and Ezekiel's Millennial Sacrifices" in *Bibliotheca Sacra* 163 (Oct.-Dec. 2006), pp. 405-22; and "Two Atonement Realms: Reconciling Sacrifice in Ezekiel and Hebrews" in *Journal of Dispensational Theology* 32 (2007), 33-64.

sacrifices. This purpose was functionally distinct from that of the redemptive work of Christ. Millennial sacrifices will not simply memorialize Christ's redemption but will primarily function in restoring and maintaining New covenant Israel in theocratic harmony. The differences between the old covenant stipulations and those of Ezekiel 40–48 can be accounted for in terms of this solution, in harmony with the unique spiritual provisions of the new covenant.

Introduction

How does the atoning work of the Lord Jesus Christ relate to the animal sacrifices God gave to Israel through Moses? What did the blood of these animals accomplish for believing and/or unbelieving Israelites during the days of the old covenant theocracy? How does that old covenant sacrificial system compare with the new covenant system envisioned in Ezekiel 40-48 and other Old Testament prophets, especially in the light of the New Testament book of Hebrews?

A wide difference of opinion still exists in this important aspect of biblical theology. It is the thesis of this study that the answers to these questions lie in the recognition that there are distinct functions in the plan of God for the blood of sacrificial animals and for the precious blood of God's Son, our Lord Jesus Christ. This distinction is especially significant for understanding the reinstatement of animal sacrifices in the future millennial kingdom of Christ.

The Church and the Mosaic Covenant

The atoning work of Jesus Christ is infinite in value and is therefore eternally sufficient and efficacious for those who put their trust in Him. This truth is clearly and repeatedly taught in the New Testament and is therefore fundamental to the

Christian faith. The book of Hebrews especially emphasizes the contrast between the substitutionary work of Christ and the blood of bulls and goats in the Mosaic/Levitical/Aaronic system of the old covenant. The following statements make this clear: "the Law made nothing perfect" (7:19); "both gifts and sacrifices are offered which cannot make the worshipper perfect in conscience" (9:9); "the Law ... can never, by the same sacrifices ... year by year, make perfect those who draw near" (10:1); "it is impossible for the blood of bulls and goats to take away sins" (10:4); "[animal] sacrifices ... can never take away sin" (10:11); "where there is forgiveness of these things, there is no longer any offering for sin" (10:18). Thus, the new covenant, in which the New Testament Church has its soteriological foundations (Heb. 8:6-13; 9:15, 12:24; cf. Luke 22:20; 1 Cor. 11:25; 2 Cor. 3:6), is infinitely superior to the old covenant of Moses, which was indeed "only a shadow of the good things to come" (Heb. 10:1).[2]

Does this mean, then, that Israel, the chosen theocratic nation, with its unconditional Abrahamic covenant guarantee of a land (Gen. 12:7; 13:14-17; 15:18-21; Deut. 30:5) and divine blessing (Gen. 12:2-3) has been forever set aside nationally in favor of the Church?[3] This has indeed been the conclusion of

---

[2] Cf. Homer A. Kent, Jr., *The Epistle to the Hebrews: A Commentary*, (Winona Lake, IN: BMH, 1972), 155-60.

[3] The Abrahamic covenant was unconditional only in the sense that God's sovereign grace guaranteed the ultimate spiritual salvation of Israel as a nation and great spiritual blessings to the nations through Abraham's ultimate Seed. It did *not* guarantee the regeneration of all his physical descendents. "An unconditional covenant ... may have blessings attached to that covenant that are conditioned upon the response of the recipient of the covenant ... but these conditional blessings do not change the unconditional character of that covenant" (J. Dwight Pentecost, *Things to Come* [Grand Rapids: Zondervan, 1964], 68). Cf. Charles C. Ryrie, *The Basis of Premillennial Faith* (New York: Loizeaux, 1953), 48-75; Eugene H. Merrill,

many Christian theologians from the days of the church fathers down to modern times. Israel as a national entity is seen by such writers as apostate and therefore broken off forever as a distinct nation in the program of God.

The New Covenant

However, the New Testament, including the book of Hebrews, does not teach that Israel has been forever set aside.[4] It does teach the end of the old covenant given by God to Israel through Moses. Yet the New Testament does not reject the Abrahamic covenant (which the new covenant of Jeremiah 31 further elaborates). During the period from the death of Christ and the Day of Pentecost to the destruction of the temple and the Jewish sacrificial system by Roman armies in AD 70, Jewish Christians were strongly pressured by their

---

"The Covenant with Abraham: The Keystone of Biblical Architecture," *Journal of Dispensational Theology* 12:36 [Aug. 2008], 5-17. The Abrahamic / New covenant and the Mosaic covenant are not in contradiction with each other. God promised, "I will put My law within them and on their heart I will write it" (Jer. 31:33; Rom. 2:25-29; 8:3-4; Heb. 7:18-19). The reappearance of *some aspects* of the Mosaic ritual during the Millennium will not necessarily, therefore, be a contradiction to the dynamics of the new covenant. This seems to harmonize with Jesus' statement in the Upper Room: "I have earnestly desired to eat this Passover with you before I suffer; for I say to you, I shall never again eat it until it is fulfilled in the kingdom of God" (Luke 22:15-16).

[4] Carefully documented refutations of "replacement theology" may be found in Ronald E. Diprose, *Israel and the Church: The Origins and Effects of Replacement Theology* (Johnson City, TN: STL Distribution, 2004); Barry E. Horner, *Future Israel: Why Christian Anti-Judaism Must Be Challenged* (Nashville: B&H Academics, 2007); Renald E. Showers, *The Coming Apocalypse* (Bellmawr, NJ: Friends of Israel, 2009); Michael J. Vlach, *Has the Church Replaced Israel?* (Nashville: B&H, 2010); and Paul Richard Wilkinson, *For Zion's Sake: Christian Zionism and the Role of John Nelson Darby* (Colorado Springs: Paternoster, 2007).

"kinsmen according to the flesh" to abandon the distinctive freedoms they found in the Christian gospel and to turn to a supposedly Mosaic legalistic belief (cf. Acts 15; Gal. 2–3). It was to such Christian believers that the author of Hebrews emphasized the shadowy insufficiency and temporary nature of the Mosaic covenant. He was not addressing old covenant national Israel, as were Jeremiah and Ezekiel, but professing members of the true Church.[5]

The contrast in Hebrews, then, is not between the Church and Israel under the new covenant or between the spiritual sacrifices offered by the Church (Heb. 13:15) and the animal sacrifices Israel will someday offer under the new covenant. It is rather between the shadowy, insufficient nature of the old covenant and the sufficient, permanent nature of the new covenant.[6] The Church participates soteriologically in the new covenant, which was originally revealed by God through Jeremiah and Ezekiel with reference to a repentant Israel in the coming kingdom age (Jer. 31:33-34; Ezek. 11:19-20; 36:25-28). The sufficiency of the new covenant is guaranteed in the spiritual regeneration of all its participants.[7]

Romans 11 and Israel's National Regeneration

The Church was graciously placed into a new covenant relationship with God, but it did not thereby replace national

---

[5] Cf. Kent, *Hebrews*, 158-59: "The author [of Hebrews] is writing to Christians when he mentions the new covenant. It is granted that they are Jewish Christians, but the fact remains that they are Christians. ... There is one new covenant to be fulfilled eschatologically with Israel, but participated in soteriologically by the church today."

[6] "New covenant" translates *diathēkēs kainēs* (διαθήκης καίυης) in Heb. 8:8; 9:15; and *diathēkēs neas* (διαθήκης νέας) in 12:24.

[7] Kent, *Hebrews*, 153.

Israel. This is explained in Romans 11:11-32. During the present age, national/theocratic Israel has indeed been rejected (v. 15) and "broken off" (vv. 17-22) because of "transgression," "failure," and "unbelief" (vv. 11, 12, 23). But that is by no means the end of Israel as a nation, for "Israel did not stumble so as to fall" (v. 11). Some day, in fact, Israel will experience divine "fulfillment" (v. 12) and "acceptance" (v. 15). Indeed, "God is able to graft them in again ... if they do not continue in their unbelief" (v. 23).

Paul argues that it will actually be more appropriate for God to do this for the "natural branches" than it was for God to graft in Gentiles "contrary to nature" (Rom. 11:24), for Israel will be grafted back into "their own olive tree" (Rom. 11:24; cf. John 4:22 – "salvation is from the Jews"). "The root" of the olive tree, which is "holy" and "rich" and which "supports" Gentile Christians, is the Abrahamic covenant (cf. Rom. 4:11-17, "the faith of Abraham, who is the father of us all").

The fact that the Church participates in the soteriological benefits of the Abrahamic and new covenants (cf. Eph. 2:12-22) is a major factor that demonstrates continuity between Israel and the Church. But it hardly demonstrates that the Church has supplanted Israel in God's program.[8] Indeed, "the

---

[8] C. E. B. Cranfield (*A Critical and Exegetical Commentary on the Epistle to the Romans.* ICC [Edinburgh: T. & T. Clark, 1981] 2:448, for example, concludes that "it is only where the Church persists in refusing to learn this message [of Romans 9–11] ... that it is unable to believe in God's mercy for still unbelieving Israel, and so entertains the ugly and unscriptural notion that God has cast off His people Israel and simply replaced it with the Christian Church. These three chapters emphatically forbid us to speak of the Church as having once and for all taken the place of the Jewish people." Then he adds in a footnote, "And I confess with shame to having also myself used in print on more than one occasion this language of the replacement of Israel by the Church." Cf. his more recent *Romans: A Shorter Commentary* (Grand Rapids: Eerdmans, 1985), 215, 273. See also John

gifts and the calling of God are irrevocable" (Rom. 11:29). Likewise, the Christian can be assured of his eternal salvation in Christ (cf. Rom. 8:28-39; Phil. 1:6) only because God keeps His covenant promises.

Israel and the New Covenant

The new covenant, originally promised to Israel as a nation (Gen. 12:1-3; Jer. 31:33-34), now also provides the Church with the infinite and eternal benefits of the substitutionary blood of Christ. But what did the new covenant originally involve? It involved God's provision for a new heart through the Holy Spirit (i.e., regeneration; cf. Ezek. 36:26-27) for the entire nation of Israel; the restoration of this regenerated nation to its ancestral land (Ezek. 36:28 – previously guaranteed by the Abrahamic covenant, and not annulled by the Mosaic covenant [Gal. 3:17]); and a dynamic, functioning theocracy of twelve tribes gathered around a great new city and temple (Ezek. 40–48; cf. Joel 3:18; Dan. 9:24; Hag. 2:7, 9; and Zech. 14:16-21). Indeed, eight centuries before the new covenant was described in detail by Jeremiah and Ezekiel, Moses, the human spokesman for the old covenant, foresaw the basic provision of the new covenant, namely a national restoration of Israel to her promised land by God's sovereign grace through regeneration of the heart (Deut. 30:1-14).

Remarkably, even the ultimate passing away of the Aaronic high priesthood for Israel was indicated at an early

---

Murray, *The Epistle to the Romans*. NICNT (Grand Rapids: Eerdmans, 1968), 2:98; and Arnold A. Van Ruler, *The Christian Church and the Old Testament* (Grand Rapids: Eerdmans, 1971) 45, 55, 57, 75-98 (extensively quoted in Earl D. Radmacher, "The Current Status of Dispensationalism and Its Eschatology" in *Perspectives on Evangelical Theology*, ed. K. S. Kantzer and S. N. Gundry [Grand Rapids: Baker, 1979], 172-74).

stage in the progress of revelation, when God announced through David concerning his great Son, a non-Levite, "Thou are a priest forever according to the order of Melchizedek" (Ps. 110:4; cf. Heb. 7). When the new covenant is fulfilled for Israel, therefore, her high priest will be none other than her Messiah, and not a descendant of Aaron. This is a fact of tremendous importance in the light of Ezekiel 40–48, which conspicuously omits any reference to a Zadokian high priest (cf. Ezek. 40:46; 43:19; 44:15; 48:11, which state that only the descendants of Zadok out of the descendants of Aaron will minister before the LORD), and the book of Hebrews, which identifies Jesus Christ as the permanent High Priest of God's people.[9]

A century before Jeremiah and Ezekiel, the prophet Isaiah also foresaw this new covenant system, even though he did not use the technical term. In the deepening gloom of national apostasy under Ahaz and even godly King Hezekiah, the prince of writing prophets spoke of "an everlasting covenant" God would make with Israel "according to the faithful mercies shown to David" (Isa. 55:3; cf. 61:8). That this anticipated the new covenant is confirmed by the fact that a national forgiveness of sin is included (59:20-21; cf. 27:9; Rom. 11:26-27). Isaiah foresaw not only God's new covenant with Israel but also a temple in the Holy Land (2:2-3; 56:5-7; 60:13). Here animal sacrifices will be offered on its altar by Egyptians (19:21) and Arabians from Kedar and Nebaioth (60:7), through "priests and Levites" (66:21), so that "the foreigners who join themselves to the Lord ... even those I [the LORD] will bring to My holy mountain and make them joyful in My house of

---

[9] See chapter 11 for a discussion of Ezekiel's emphasis on Zadokian priests in the future temple.

prayer. Their burnt offerings and their sacrifices will be acceptable on My altar" (56:6-7; cf. 66:19-20).

To Hosea, Isaiah's contemporary prophet in the northern kingdom, the wonders of this great new covenant were also revealed (Hos. 2:14-23). Hosea implied that after "many days" during which the nation would be "without king or prince," animal "sacrifices" would be resumed "in the last days" (3:4-5).

Jeremiah lived to see the final collapse of the politically independent theocracy of Israel (609–586 BC). To him the expression "a new covenant" was first revealed. This new covenant included the offering of animals upon the altar of a temple in the Holy Land. Looking back to the Davidic covenant (which was one aspect of the Abrahamic covenant), the God of Israel announced, "I will cause a righteous Branch of David to spring forth ... David shall never lack a man to sit on the throne of the house of Israel" (33:15, 17; cf. vv. 21, 22, 26). Then he added these significant words: "and the Levitical priests shall never lack a man before Me to offer burnt offerings, to burn grain offerings and to prepare sacrifices continually" (33:18; cf. vv. 21, 22). Thus, Jeremiah, in stating the total demise of the temporary old covenant (31:32), and in anticipating the national regeneration provided in the permanent new covenant (31:31-34; 32:38-40; 33:6-13; 50:5), included animal sacrifices offered by Levitical priests as permanent aspects of this new covenant for national Israel.

Ezekiel was the third major prophet who spoke of Israel's everlasting covenant of peace: designated in 16:60-63; 20:37; 34:25; 37:21-28; and described soteriologically in 11:19-20 and 36:25-28. Included in this covenant was provision for "My sanctuary in their midst forever" (37:26, 28). In amazing detail, this sanctuary or temple is then described in chapters 40-48 with regard to (1) the precise dimensions and arrangements of its courts, gates, chambers, and furnishings (40:5–43:27); (2) its officials, including the mortal prince (44:3; 45:7, 16, 22; 46:2-18) and the Levitical descendants of Zadok (who replaced Abiathar as David's faithful high priest), who would serve as priests (40:46; 43:19; 44:10-31; 48:11); (3) the different types and characteristics and purposes of its animal sacrifices (40:38-43; 42:13; 43:18-27; 44:11-16, 27-29; 45:15-25; 46:2-15; 46:20-24; cf. 20:40); and (4) the boundaries and dimensions of the tribal territories surrounding the city and the temple with its life-giving river (47:1–48:35).

Zechariah foresaw the strict enforcement of the Feast of Tabernacles among all Gentile nations (14:16-19; cf. Ezek. 45:25). Zechariah also anticipated, in connection with the fulfillment of the new covenant (9:11; 13:1), that "all who sacrifice will come and take [every cooking pot in Jerusalem] and boil in them" (14:21). Other prophets who spoke of the future temple were Joel (3:18), Micah (4:1-5), Daniel (9:24), Haggai (2:7, 9), and Malachi (3:3-4). Our Lord referred to this temple in Matthew 24:15 (cf. Mark 13:14); Paul in 2 Thessalonians 2:4; and John in Revelation 11:1-2.

The Church and the New Covenant

How should Christian participants in the new covenant view these prophetic utterances concerning a restoration of national Israel to its land, complete with temple, Zadokian priests, and animal sacrifices, especially in the light of the emphatic pronouncements of the book of Hebrews? Liberal and Neo-orthodox theologians dismiss Ezekiel's temple vision as an apocalyptic dream[10] or a tentative plan for the second

---

[10] Cf. Moshe Greenberg, "The Design and Themes of Ezekiel's Program of Restoration," *Interpretation* 38 (1984), 181-208; John W. Wevers, *Ezekiel. The New Century Bible Commentary* (Grand Rapids: Eerdmans, 1969), 207; and

temple, which the returning exiles never adopted.[11] Most evangelical commentators assume that the covenants of God with Israel are being fulfilled in the Church[12] and/or refer somehow to the eternal state.[13] Even some premillennialists, finding it difficult to reconcile animal sacrifices in the Millennium with the book of Hebrews, conclude that Israel's new covenant will indeed eventuate in national conversion and divine blessing in the Holy Land for a thousand years, but without a temple, priests, and sacrifices.[14]

Jon Douglas Levenson, *Theology of the Program of Restoration of Ezekiel 40–48* (Missoula, MT: Scholars, 1976), 161-63. Surprisingly, this position is also advocated by John B. Taylor, *Ezekiel: An Introduction and Commentary* (London: Tyndale, 1969), 253.

[11] Among those who have held this view are Eichhorn, Dathe, Herder, Doederlein, and Hitzig. These are cited in Patrick Fairbairn, *An Exposition of Ezekiel* (Evansville, IN: Sovereign Grace, reprint 1960), 433.

[12] Cf. Fairbairn, *Ezekiel*, 435: "From the Fathers downward this has been the prevailing view in the Christian Church." See also Andrew W. Blackwood, Jr., *Ezekiel: Prophecy of Hope* (Grand Rapids: Baker, 1965), 235, 270. Typical of Blackwood's dubious hermeneutics is his discussion of the centrality of the altar in Ezek. 40:17: "Many Protestants today are carefully ignoring God's message to us through Ezekiel's placement of the altar. ... Today in the beautiful new Roman Catholic churches that are being constructed the sacramental table is brought away from the wall; so that the congregation, insofar as it is physically possible, surrounds the table. Ezekiel certainly is telling us that church architecture should be an expression of theology" (pp. 240-41).

[13] Cf. Anthony A. Hoekema, *The Bible and the Future* (Grand Rapids: Eerdmans, 1979) 205-6; H. L. Ellison, *Ezekiel: The Man and His Message* (Grand Rapids: Eerdmans, 1956), 137-44; and C. F. Keil, *Commentary on the Old Testament* (Grand Rapids: Zondervan, reprint n.d.), 9:417. However, for a list of contrasts between Ezekiel 40–48 and Revelation 21–22, see Ralph Alexander, *Ezekiel* (Chicago: Moody, 1970), 130-32.

[14] Cf. Increase Mather, *The Mystery of Israel's Salvation*, vol. 22 in *A Library of American Puritan Writings*, ed. Sacvan Bercovitch (New York: AMS, 1983), 113-14; George N. H. Peters, *The Theocratic Kingdom* (Grand Rapids: Kregel,

Keenly sensitive to the tensions and the problems involved in this theological controversy, John F. Walvoord significantly concluded that "the most thoroughgoing students of pre-millennialism who evince understanding of the relation of literal interpretation to premillennial doctrine usually embrace the concept of a literal temple and literal sacrifices."[15] Without doubt, the large majority of dispensational premillennialists do interpret the Zadokian priesthood and animal sacrifices of the millennial age literally. They also attempt to modify the supposed clash between the Old Testament prophecies of the new covenant and the book of Hebrews by viewing these animal sacrifices strictly as memorials of the death of Christ, like the church Eucharist of the bread and cup.[16] Such an approach may be questioned, however.

---

reprint 1952), 3, 83-91; H. A. Ironside, *Ezekiel the Prophet* (New York: Loizeaux, 1949), 284-90; and J. Sidlow Baxter, *Explore the Book* (Grand Rapids: Zondervan, 1960), 4:32. In contrast, Erich Sauer (*From Eternity to Eternity* [Grand Rapids: Eerdmans, 1954], 181) has provided a wholesome perspective on the basic hermeneutical issue: "*Either* the prophet himself was mistaken in his expectation of a coming temple service, and the prophecy in the sense in which he himself meant it will never be fulfilled; *or* God, in the time of the Messiah, will fulfill literally these prophecies of the temple according to their intended literal meaning. There is no other choice possible."

[15] John F. Walvoord, *The Millennial Kingdom* (Findlay, OH: Dunham, 1959), 315; cf. p. 311.

[16] Cf. Walvoord, *The Millennial Kingdom*, 312. Progressive revelation requires that millennial believers (who will constitute a decreasing proportion of the world's population as the kingdom age continues) will be reminded of the sacrifice of the Lamb of God when they behold the shedding of animal blood at the Temple altar. Cf. Arno C. Gaebelein, *The Prophet Ezekiel* (New York: Our Hope, 1918), 311-13. However, that will not be their *sole* purpose and function.

The key to the entire problem may be found in answers to three questions. (1) What was the true function of animal sacrifices in the old covenant? (2) What is the significance of the fundamental differences between Ezekiel's picture of the new covenant system of worship and the old covenant system of worship? (3) Would a worship system involving animal sacrifices necessarily represent a great step backward for new covenant Israel during the kingdom Age?

The True Function of Animal Sacrifices

In answer to the first question, animal sacrifices could never remove spiritual guilt from the offerer or clear his conscience. The book of Hebrews is very clear about that (10:4, 11). But it is equally erroneous to say that the sacrifices were mere teaching symbols given by God to Israel to prepare them for Messiah and His infinite atonement. Such a view is contradicted by precise statements in Exodus and Leviticus.[17]

The Scriptures tell us that something really did happen to the Israelite offerer when he came to the right altar with the appropriate sacrifice; and he was expected to know what would happen to him. What happened was temporal, finite, external, and legal – not external, infinite, internal, and soteri-

---

[17] Cf. John S. Feinberg, "Salvation in the Old Testament," in *Tradition and Testament: Essays in Honor of Charles Lee Feinberg,* ed. John S. and Paul D. Feinberg, (Chicago: Moody, 1981), 70. Cf. Charles C. Ryrie, *Dispensationalism* (Chicago: Moody, 1995), 117-120. Ryrie correctly concludes: "The basis of salvation is always the death of Christ; the means is always faith; the object is always God (though man's understanding of God before and after the incarnation is obviously different); but the content of faith depends on the particular revelation God was pleased to give at a certain time. These are the distinctions which the dispensationalist recognizes, and they are distinctions necessitated by plain interpretation of revelation as it was given" (121).

ological. Nevertheless, what happened was personally and immediately significant, not simply symbolic and/or prophetic. When an Israelite "unwittingly failed" to observe a particular ordinance of the Mosaic Law (in the weakness of his sin nature [Num. 15:22-29], not "defiantly," in open rebellion against God Himself [Num. 15:30-36]),[18] he was actually "forgiven" through an "atonement" (a ritual cleansing; cf. Heb. 9:10, 13) made by the priest (Num. 15:25-26).

But what was the precise nature of this "forgiveness" and this "atonement"? To say that it was exclusively a prophetic anticipation of Christ's atoning work does not do justice to the progress of revelation.[19] There simply is no biblical evidence that the knowledge-content of Old Testament saving faith always and necessarily included a crucified Messiah. However, in God's eternal purpose, the death of His Son has always been and always will be the final basis of spiritual salvation (Rom. 3:25-26). Saving faith before the Day of Pentecost (Acts 2) involved a heart response to whatever special revelation of God was available at that time in history (cf. Rom. 4; Gal. 3; Heb. 11). Such Spirit-initiated faith produced a "circumcised heart" (Lev. 26:41; Deut. 10:16; 30:6; Jer. 4:4; 9:25; Ezek. 44:7, 9). No one was ever spiritually regenerated by works, not even by fulfilling legally prescribed sacrifices, offerings, and other Mosaic requirements.[20]

---

[18] Cf. Walter C. Kaiser, Jr., *Toward an Old Testament Theology* (Grand Rapids: Zondervan, 1978), 117-18.

[19] Cf. John S. Feinberg, "Salvation in the Old Testament," 50, 51, 53, 55, 68. See also Ryrie, *Dispensationalism*, 118-119: "Unquestionably the Old Testament does ascribe efficacy to the sacrifices. ... The bringing of sacrifices restored the offender to his forfeited position as a Jewish worshipper and restored his theocratic relationship."

[20] John S. Feinberg, "Salvation in the Old Testament," 61.

In the covenant at Sinai, God provided a highly complex and rigid structure for his "kingdom of priests." Within that structure, national/theocratic transgressions would receive national/theocratic forgiveness when appropriate sacrifices were offered to God through legitimate priests at the tabernacle/temple altar. This "forgiveness" was promised regardless of the spiritual state of either the offerer or the priest. For example, in anticipation of the Sinai covenant about to be revealed through Moses, God made this amazing promise to the entire nation of Israel in Egypt – both believers and unbelievers – at the time of the Exodus: "When I see the blood [on your two doorposts and on the lintel] I will pass over you" (Exod. 12:13; cf. 12:23). Note carefully that the Lord did not say, "I will forgive all your sins." Most of them continued to be unbelievers! The promise was to protect them from immediate destruction: "The Lord will pass over the door and will not allow the destroyer to come in to your houses to smite you" (Exod. 12:23).

Sacrificial blood could never cleanse the conscience or save the soul (Heb. 10:1-2), so God repeatedly sent prophets to call His people to love and obey their God from the heart. Apart from such genuine faith, all the ceremonially "kosher" animals in the whole world would avail nothing in the spiritual realm (Ps. 50:7-15; Isa. 1:11-20; Amos 4:4-5; 5:21-27; Hos. 5:6; Mic. 6:6-8; Jer. 6:20; 7:21-23). It was not to be either faith or sacrifices; rather, it was to be both faith and sacrifices (cf. Ps. 51:19).

It was just as true then as it is today: "It is impossible for the blood of bulls and goats to take away sins" (Heb. 10:4). But it was also true then, under the old covenant, that "the blood of goats and bulls ... sanctify for the cleansing of the flesh" (Heb. 9:13). In the words of F. F. Bruce,

> The blood of slaughtered animals under the old
> order did possess a certain efficacy, but it was an
> outward efficacy for the removal of ceremonial
> pollution. ... They could restore [the worship-
> per] to formal communion with God and with
> fellow-worshippers. ... Just how the blood of
> sacrificed animals or the ashes of a red heifer
> effected a ceremonial cleansing our author does
> not explain; it was sufficient for him, and no
> doubt for his readers, that the Old Testament
> ascribed this efficacy to them.[21]

This was the unique tension within the theocracy of Israel that many Christian theologians apparently do not comprehend.

Now what does all of this indicate with regard to animal sacrifices in the millennial temple for Israel under the new covenant? It indicates that future sacrifices will have nothing to do with eternal salvation, which comes only through true faith in God. It also indicates that future animal sacrifices will be "efficacious" and "expiatory" only in terms of the strict provision for ceremonial (and thus temporal) forgiveness within the theocracy of Israel. Thus, animal sacrifices during the coming kingdom age will not be primarily memorial, like the bread and the cup ("do this in remembrance of Me," 1 Cor.

---

[21] F. F. Bruce, *The Epistle to the Hebrews.* NICNT (Grand Rapids: Eerdmans, 1964), 201, 204, italics added. In a personal communication, Professor John A. Sproule noted that "to argue from the present tense of *hagiazei* in Hebrews 9:13 that such things (i.e., the blood of bulls and goats and the sprinkling of the ashes of the heifer) would still sanctify defiled persons, as such ceremonies might still be carried out in Jewish sects at the time during which the author of Hebrews was writing, is unnecessary. The present tense (aspect) in New Testament Greek is much more flexible. The tense ... could be used here simply for dramatic effect or vividness."

11:24), in church Communion services, any more than sacrifices in the age of the old covenant were primarily prospective or prophetic in the understanding of the offerer.

It is at this point that premillennial theologians exhibit differences. A. C. Gaebelein expressed, perhaps, the majority opinion when he wrote: "While the sacrifices Israel brought once had a prospective meaning, the sacrifices brought in the millennial temple have a retrospective meaning."[22] Ezekiel, however, does not say that animals will be offered for a "memorial" of Messiah's death. Rather, they will be for "atonement" (45:15, 17, 20; cf. 43:20, 26).

> The Hebrew word used to describe the purpose of these sacrifices in Ezekiel 45:15, 17, and 20 is the piel form of kaphar. ... But this is precisely the word used in the Pentateuchal description of the OT sacrifices to indicate their ... expiatory purpose (cf. Lev. 6:30; 8:15; 16:6, 11, 24, 30, 32, 33, 34; Num. 5:8; 15:28; 29:5). If the sacrifices mentioned in Ezekiel are to be understood literally, they must be expiatory, not memorial offerings.[23]

---

[22] Gaebelein, *The Prophet Ezekiel,* 312. For a listing and analysis of other nineteenth- and early twentieth-century proponents of literal sacrifices in the Millennium (e.g., Adolph Saphir, William Kelly, Nathanael West, W. Haslam, Burlington B. Wade, John Fry, and H. Bonar), cf. John L. Mitchell, "The Question of Millennial Sacrifices," Bibliotheca Sacra 110 (1953), 248-67. George N. H. Peters (*The Theocratic Kingdom,* 3, 83, 88) also mentions D. N. Lord, Tyso, Shimeall, Begg, Baumgarten (in Herzog's *Encyclopedia,* "Ezekiel"), Auberlen, Hofman, and Volch.

[23] Hoekema, *The Bible and the Future,* 204, n. 16. As we have already explained, "expiatory" is the wrong term to describe the function of these sacrifices, if the term is understood on the infinite level of Christ's work on the Cross.

The distinction between ceremonial and spiritual atonement is by no means a minor one, for it is at the heart of the basic difference between the theocracy of Israel and the Church, the body and bride of Christ. It also provides a more consistent hermeneutical approach for dispensational premillennialism.

In his analysis of atonement in the Old Testament, Richard E. Averbeck has shown that the Hebrew term *kapar*, used so frequently in Leviticus, does not mean "to cover" but rather "to appease or cleanse."

> Only Christ's sacrifice was of the kind that could form the basis for eternal and spiritual salvation (Heb. 9:15). But this in no way refutes the ... efficacy in the Old Testament atonement sacrifices. Those sacrifices had to do with the covenant relationship between God and the nation of Israel. Eternal or spiritual salvation was not the issue. Therefore, the animal sacrifices of the Old Testament and the sacrifice of Christ in the New Testament were effective at their own respective [and totally different] levels.[24]

With respect to the Millennium, Averbeck concludes:

> This accords well with the issue of the millennial sacrifices mentioned in Ezekiel. These rituals will not be memorials. They will atone ... in the same efficacious way as the ones in Aaronic times. Why will this be necessary? Because God

---

[24] Richard E. Averbeck, "An Exegetical Study of Leviticus 1:4 with a Discussion of the Nature of Old Testament Atonement" (M.Div. thesis; Grace Theological Seminary, 1977), 68.

will again be dwelling, in His glory, among [mortal] men. ... Christ did not shed His blood for the cleansing of any physical altar. Therefore, the special rite for the yearly cleansing of the millennial sanctuary will be required (Ezek. 45:18-20). Regular sacrifices will be reinstituted in the millennium.[25]

In the light of these considerations, it is significant that Anthony A. Hoekema, an amillennial theologian, leveled one of his heaviest criticisms of premillennialism at this very point.

Extremely significant is the note on page 888 of the New Scofield Bible which suggests the following as a possible interpretation of the sacrifices mentioned in these chapters of Ezekiel's prophecy: "The reference to sacrifices is not to be taken literally, in view of the putting away of such offerings, but is rather to be regarded as a presentation of the worship of redeemed Israel, in her own land and in the millennial temple, using the terms with which the Jews were familiar in Ezekiel's day." These words convey a far-reaching concession on the part of dispensationalists. If the sacrifices are not to be taken literally, why should we take the temple literally? It would seem that the dispensational principle of the literal interpretation of Old Testament prophecy is here abandoned, and that

---

[25] Ibid., 68-69. In a personal communication (Feb. 1985), Averbeck suggested that the "cleansing of the sanctuary" (= "you shall make atonement for the house") during the *first* week of the *first* month constitutes the millennial form of the ancient Day of Atonement.

a crucial foundation stone for the entire dispensational system has here been set aside![26]

Hoekema's objection is well taken. However, he assumes, along with many nondispensational theologians, that animal sacrifices in the Millennium will involve a reinstitution of the Mosaic economy, just as if Christ had never died. Oswald T. Allis, another Reformed theologian, stated, for example: "Literally interpreted, this means the restoration of the Aaronic priesthood and the Mosaic ritual of sacrifices essentially unchanged."[27] That this is not the case will be demonstrated next.

Israelite Worship Under the Old and New Covenants Contrasted

Ezekiel's picture of millennial worship and the Mosaic system, which had been established nine hundred years earlier, exhibit fundamental differences. Old Testament scholars have often wrestled with the significance of these differences. Andrew W. Blackwood Jr. did not hesitate to call them "discrepancies," hastening to assure his readers that

> they concern matters that make no earthly difference to Christian faith, however they may have jarred the sensibilities of our Jewish forebears. There are twenty major discrepancies be-

---

[26] Hoekema, *The Bible and the Future,* 204. The footnote cited by Hoekema in *The New Scofield Reference Bible* ([New York: Oxford, 1967], 888, n. 1) actually offers this view as the second of "two answers" to the animal sacrifice problem in Ezek. 43:19 that "have been suggested." It was, nevertheless, a serious concession.

[27] Oswald T. Allis, *Prophecy and the Church* (Philadelphia: Presbyterian and Reformed, 1945), 246; cf. 245, 248.

tween Ezekiel and the Torah. Compare 46:6f.
with Numbers 28:11, for example. Here are
outright contradictions in the number of bul-
locks, lambs and rams and the amount of flour
to be used at the new moon offering ceremonies.
... Long ago the rabbis were driven to say that
Elijah, when he came, would explain away the
difficulties. They said likewise that the entire
prophecy would have been excluded from the
canon were it not for the devoted labor of Rabbi
Hanina ben Hezekiah, a scholar of the first
century A.D., who must have written an extensive commentary on Ezekiel: "Three hundred
barrels of oil were provided for him [for light],
and he sat in an upper chamber where he reconciled all discrepancies" (Babylonian Talmud,
Menahoth 45a).[28]

It is the view of the present study that there are no discrepancies within Scripture and that God's servants today do
not have to wait until Elijah appears to discover a theologically and hermeneutically satisfactory solution to this
problem.

A century ago, Nathanael West listed some of the important differences between old covenant Israel and millennial
Israel in order to show how appropriate Ezekiel's structure
will be for the kingdom age.

If the similarities between [Ezekiel's] portrait of
the "many days" of Israel in the Kingdom, and
Israel's former Old Testament life, their ritual
and laws, are remarkable, still more remarkable

---

[28] Blackwood, *Ezekiel: Prophecy of Hope*, 21-22.

are the vast and important differences noted by Jews and Christians alike; differences so great as to make the [Jews], at one time, almost extrude the book from the sacred canon as uninspired. It is plain that these differences imply an entire revolution from the old order of things, and intimate strongly the "vanishing away" of the Law, to make room for the "new covenant" he has elsewhere, like Jeremiah, Hosea, and Isaiah, proclaimed with such spiritual force.

There are changes in the dimensions of the Temple so that it is neither the temple of Solomon, nor that of Zerubbabel, nor that of Herod; changes in the measures of the outer court, the gates, the walls, the grounds, and the locality of the temple itself, raised on a high mountain, and even separate from the City. The Holy Places have hardly anything like the furniture that stood in the Tabernacle of Moses or the Temple of Solomon.

There are subtractions also. There is no Ark of the Covenant [cf. Jer. 3:16], no Pot of Manna, no Aaron's Rod to bud, no Tables of the Law, no Cherubim, no Mercy-Seat, no Golden Candlestick, no Showbread, no Veil, no unapproachable Holy of Holies where the High Priest alone might enter, nor is there any High Priest. ... The priesthood is confined to the sons of Zadok, and only for a special purpose. There is no evening sacrifice. ... The social, moral, and civil pre-

scriptions enforced by Moses with such emphasis are all wanting.[29]

William Kelly was fascinated with the fact that there will
be nothing in the Millennium answering to the Feast of Pentecost.

> The omission seems to me to denote how com-
> pletely it has been realized in the highest sense
> in the Church, which, as it were, has monopo-
> lized it. That heavenly body has come in
> between the true Passover, and before the
> verification of the Tabernacles [cf. Ezek. 45:25;
> Zech. 14:16-19], and has, so to speak, absorbed
> Pentecost to itself. ... Who but God Himself
> could have thought of such an omission as that
> of Pentecost six centuries before it was realized
> so unexpectedly after the ascension?[30]

In addition to all of this, C. F. Keil, writing from a post-
millennial perspective, discovered ceremonial and ritual
adaptations in Ezekiel's vision of Israel's future service for
God that he believed to be far more appropriate than the
Mosaic structure for a post-Calvary eschatological program.

> According to Ezekiel's order of feasts and sac-
> rifices, Israel was to begin every new year of its
> life with a great sin-offering on the first, seventh,
> and fourteenth days of the first month ... before
> it renewed the covenant of grace with the Lord

---

[29] Nathanael West, *The Thousand Years in Both Testaments* (New York: Revell, 1880), 429-30.

[30] William Kelly, *Lectures on the Second Coming of Our Lord Jesus Christ*, 267-69. Quoted in John L. Mitchell, "The Question of Millennial Sacrifices," 260.

in the paschal meal ... and throughout the year consecrate its life to the Lord in the daily burnt-offering, through increased Sabbath-offerings ... in order to live before Him a blameless, righteous, and happy life.[31]

Keil also concluded that the shift "of the chief atoning sacrifices" from the seventh month, at the end of the religious year, to the first month (for Ezekiel completely eliminates the Feast of Trumpets and the Day of Atonement, leaving only the Feast of Tabernacles in the seventh month)

indicates that, for the Israel of the new covenant, this eternally-availing atoning sacrifice would form the foundation for all its acts of worship and keeping of feasts, as well as for the whole course of its life. It is in this that we find the Messianic feature of Ezekiel's order of sacrifices and feasts, by which it acquires a character more in accordance with the New Testament completion of the sacrificial service, which also presents itself to us in the other and still more deeply penetrating modifications of the Mosaic torah of sacrifice on the part of Ezekiel [which] indicates that the people offering these sacrifices will bring forth more of the fruit of sanctification in good works upon the ground of the reconciliation which it has received.[32]

These are helpful insights, almost unique to a non-premillennial commentator, for understanding the religious

---

[31] C. F. Keil, *Commentary on the Old Testament: Ezekiel* (Grand Rapids: Eerdmans, reprint n.d.), 429.

[32] Ibid., 430.

structure of the millennial kingdom age as well as the function of animal sacrifices during that time period. Unfortunately, Keil's theological position forced him to abandon the literal fulfillment of these prophecies and to denounce "M. Baumgarten, Auberlen, and other millenarians [who] express the opinion that this shadow-work will be restored after the eventual conversion of Israel to Christ, in support of which Baumgarten even appeals to the authority of the apostle to the Gentiles [Romans 11]."[33]

Millennial Sacrifices Will Not Be a Backward Step for Israel

Consistent dispensationalism must teach the practice of animal sacrifices for a restored and regenerated Israel in the Millennium. But this raises the third major question: Would such a worship system necessarily represent a great step backward for new covenant Israel during the kingdom age?

The answer is no, for Israel will indeed be under a new covenant program, not the old covenant given to Moses, which was not designed to guarantee salvation. Church Communion services will no longer be observed, for they have been designed only to "proclaim the Lord's death until He comes" (1 Cor. 11:26). But after He comes, animal sacrifices within a new covenant structure, endorsed (though not performed; cf. John 4:2) by the living Lamb of God, will constitute a gigantic step forward for Israel, not a reversion to "weak and worthless elements" (Gal. 4:9) that actually enslaved the nation because of its unregenerate misuse of the Law. The apostle Paul "did not see any contradiction between

---

[33] Ibid., 431.

the finished work of Christ and the offering of animal sacrifice" (Acts 21:26).[34]

John A. Sproule has pointed to the principle of progressive revelation as a guarantee that millennial Israel will have the entire New Testament available to them, including the book of Hebrews.[35] The two witnesses (Rev. 11), the 144,000 (Rev. 7, 14), and the Zadokian teaching priests functioning in the millennial temple (Ezekiel 40–48) will therefore know considerably more than John the Baptist, Apollos, the apostle Paul (who probably never read the book of Revelation), and even the apostle John. They will know about the full and finished work of the Lord Jesus Christ. They will see no conflict between Ezekiel and Hebrews. They will realize that the omission of a high priest in Ezekiel 40–48 was not a mistake, just as it is now realized that the omission of a genealogy for Melchizedek in Genesis 14 was not a mistake (cf. Heb. 7).[36] Rather, they will recognize this omission as God's way of opening the door to the Melchizedekian High Priest of Psalm 110:4 (cf. Zech. 6:13: "He will be a priest on His throne"), whose visible presence on earth during the coming kingdom age will be the ultimate answer to this dilemma of the ages.

Believing Jews will experience regeneration and sanctification (but not Spirit baptism), just as Christians do today,

---

[34] Hullinger, "A Proposed Solution to the Problem of Animal Sacrifices in Ezekiel 40–48," 230; cf. pp. 10 and 232.

[35] John A. Sproule, personal communication with the author, February, 1985.

[36] For additional insights on this important issue, see Randall Price, *The Temple and Bible Prophecy* (Eugene, OR: Harvest House, 2005), 516-57; Thomas Ice, "Literal Sacrifices in the Millennium," *Pre-Trib Perspectives* (June, 2000), 4-5; and Arnold G. Fruchtenbaum, *The Footsteps of the Messiah* (Tustin, CA: Ariel Ministries, 2003), 458-69.

by the grace of God and through faith in the Lord Jesus. These future Jewish believers and their Gentile proselytes will not be glorified through seeing Jesus at His coming and in His kingdom any more than the disciples in the Upper Room were glorified when they saw their resurrected Lord. However, the concept of progressive revelation guarantees that the new covenant theocracy will begin with more knowledge than the Church had at Pentecost. Yet this theocracy will retain its distinctive Israelite characteristics – a Promised Land, a temple, appropriate animal sacrifices, and an earthly Zadokian priesthood (in that day visibly subordinate to Jesus Christ, the Melchizedekian High Priest).

These sacrifices, illumined by a vastly greater understanding of the true significance of the Lamb of God who has taken away the sin of the world, will be appreciated all the more for what they can and cannot accomplish for the offerer. For nonglorified millennial Israel and her Gentile proselytes throughout the world (e.g., Ps. 87; Isa. 60:1-14; Zech. 8:20-23), the continued presence of a sin nature will call for constant instruction and exhortation in revealed truth. Not even a perfect government will automatically solve this deep, universal problem.

Jerry M. Hullinger concludes:

> The fundamental rationale of the Mosaic sacrificial system [was] the presence of the divine glory. The Mosaic system was instituted in Leviticus subsequent to the descent of the Shekinah in Exodus 40:34-38. Because of the communicability of uncleanness, the purity of God's presence needed to be protected. Fittingly, as Ezekiel envisioned a future temple in the millennial kingdom with the resident glory of God [Ezek.

43:2-7; 44:1-4], he saw the necessity of sacrificial blood once more because of the presence of nonglorified individuals who can be a source of communicable contamination.[37]

In distinction from the perfection of the eternal state as described in Revelation 21–22, Christ will "rule all the nations with a rod of iron" (Rev. 12:5; cf. 2:27; 19:15) with strict controls, especially in religious practices (cf. Zech. 14:16-21). Even though outward submission to these religious forms will not necessarily demonstrate a regenerate heart (which has been true in every age of human history), it will guarantee protection from physical penalties and temporal judgments. Those who love the Christ will exhibit a genuine spirit of submission to His government. But those who do not truly love Him will follow Satan (even Judas Iscariot betrayed Christ after years of observing His perfect leadership) in global rebellion at the end of His righteous reign and will be destroyed in cosmic fire (Rev. 20:7-9).

Conclusion

How can vital spiritual instruction be accomplished for citizens of the millennial kingdom age through a system of animal sacrifices? If it is theoretically possible (though sadly rare) for the Church today to achieve a spiritual, symbolic, and pedagogic balance in the use of the bread and the cup in the Eucharist, then it will be all the more possible for

---

[37] Hullinger, "The Divine Presence, Uncleanness, and Ezekiel's Millennial Sacrifices," 422. Cf. Hullinger, "The Problem of Animal Sacrifices in Ezekiel 40–48," 281; and Jerry Hullinger, "The Compatibility of the New Covenant and Future Animal Sacrifice," *Journal of Dispensational Theology* 17:50 (Spring, 2013): 47-64.

regenerated Israel to attain the divinely intended balance between form and content, lip and heart, hand and soul, within the structures of the new covenant. It is not only possible, but prophetically certain, that millennial animal sacrifices will be used in a God-honoring way (e.g., Ps. 51:15-19; Heb. 11:4) by a regenerated, chosen nation before the inauguration of the eternal state, when animals will presumably no longer exist.

Before the heavens and the earth flee away from him who sits upon the Great White Throne (Rev. 20:11), God will provide a final demonstration of the validity of animal sacrifices as an instructional and disciplinary instrument for Israel. The entire world will see the true purpose of this system. Of course, the system never has and never will function on the level of Calvary's Cross, where infinite and eternal guilt was dealt with once and for all. But the system did accomplish, under God, some very important pedagogical and disciplinary purposes for Israel under the old covenant (Gal. 4:1-7). There is good reason to believe that it will yet again, and far more successfully from a pedagogical standpoint, function on the level of purely temporal cleansing and forgiveness (cf. Heb. 9:13) within the strict limits of the national theocracy of Israel during the one thousand years of Christ's reign upon the earth in accordance with the terms of the new covenant.

13

The Thousand-Year Reign of Christ over the Earth

The Universal and Mediatorial Kingdoms of God

I thank God upon every remembrance of my theological/ eschatological mentor, Dr. Alva J. McClain. At Grace Theological Seminary, he was my teacher (1948-51) and my esteemed colleague (1951-68). One of my greatest privileges was to assist him in the publication of his masterpiece, *The Greatness of the Kingdom.*

Dr. McClain was especially helpful in distinguishing between the *universal* kingdom of God and the *mediatorial* kingdom. The former is what has always existed; is universal in scope, outside of which is no created thing; involves the rule of God directly, with no intermediary standing between God and man; is a present reality; and is an unconditioned rule, arising out of the sovereign nature of God Himself.[1]

---

[1] Alva J. McClain, *The Greatness of the Kingdom* (Winona Lake, IN: BMH, 1974), 19-20. See also Mark A. Snoeberger, "Distinctive Contributions of Alva J. McClain and Grace Theological Seminary to a History of Dispensationalism," *Detroit Baptist Theological Seminary Journal* 17 (2012), 35-61.

In contrast, the mediatorial kingdom "must 'come' to put down at last all rebellion with its train of evil results, thus finally bringing the Kingdom and will of God *on* earth as it is in heaven. ... The King of this kingdom is the Lord Jesus, the Son of David; the subjects of it are Israel and the nations ... the center of the kingdom is Jerusalem, and the means of its establishment is the coming and visible appearing of our Saviour Jesus Christ."[2]

The Thousand-Year Reign of Christ

This is "the kingdom" the Jews were looking for but, sadly, on their own terms! That was their final stumbling block— they had to repent! "Now in those days John the Baptist came, preaching in the wilderness of Judea, saying, 'Repent, for the kingdom of heaven [i.e., the mediatorial kingdom] is at hand'" (Matt. 3:1-2). Then our Lord Himself "began to preach and say, 'Repent, for the kingdom of heaven is at hand'" (Matt. 4:17). And that was the message of the Twelve as well (Mark 6:12; Acts 2:38; 3:19), and the apostle Paul (Acts 17:30; 26:20), in obedience to our Lord's command "that repentance for forgiveness of sins would be proclaimed in His name to all the nations, beginning from Jerusalem" (Luke 24:47).

The Jews wanted the kingdom, especially to liberate them from the oppression of Rome. But the vast majority of the nation—especially the leaders—despised the divine condition of repentance! They were shocked and offended at the suggestion that they needed to experience a profound change of attitude regarding their need of a Savior from sin in order to enter God's holy kingdom. That is why they killed John the Baptist and, finally, their own Messiah!

---

[2] McClain, *The Greatness of the Kingdom*, 35.

So, the inauguration of the mediatorial kingdom of Christ was contingent upon the repentance of the nation. How sad! "Jerusalem … How often I wanted to gather your children together … and you were unwilling. Behold, your house is left to you desolate! … from now on you will not see Me until you say, 'Blessed is He who comes in the Name of the LORD!'" (Matt. 23:37-39).

Note carefully: The Lord Jesus did not say, "From now on you will not see Me." What He did say is amazing: "You will not see Me until you say, 'Blessed is He …'" Will Israel as a nation ever say that to their Messiah? Yes! Note these words God gave to the apostle Paul: " I do not want you, brethren, to be uninformed of this mystery—so that you will not be wise in your own estimation—that a partial [not complete!] hardening has happened to Israel until [not permanently!] the fullness of the Gentiles has come in; and so all Israel [not the Church!] will be saved" (Rom. 11:25-26).

Basic Characteristics of the Mediatorial Kingdom[3]

When will the kingdom come, and what will it be like? Consider these sixteen characteristics.

(1) Glorified men will serve as kings and also as Melchizedekian-type priests under Christ.

Resurrected and raptured Christians (the true glorified Church, represented by the twenty-four elders of Rev. 4, 5, 19), now officially married to the Lamb (Rev. 19:7-9), will share His throne (Rev. 3:21) in judging both angels and men (1 Cor. 6:2-3) at His second coming. Their "thrones" thus will be

---

[3] This section is taken largely from the author's plastic-coated chart, "The Thousand-Year Reign of Christ over the Earth" (Winona Lake, IN: BMH Books, 2010).

extensions of Christ's millennial, Davidic throne (Luke 1:32; cf. Rev. 2:26-27). When Messiah/Christ sets foot on the Mount of Olives (Zech. 14:4), pre-Pentecost and post-rapture, Antichrist-martyred "Israelites indeed," including their Gentile prose-lytes (Isa. 19:23-25), will be resurrected and glorified (Dan. 12:1-3). Generally invisible to earth dwellers (like angels today), they will serve as "kings" under Christ (and His Church) for a thousand years (Rev. 20:4) over nonglorified Is-raelite and Gentile rulers on the earth (Ps. 149:5-9; Isa. 32:1; 53:12; Ezek. 46:16-18; Dan. 7:18, 22, 27; Luke 19:17, 19).

All glorified saints also will serve as "priests" (Rev. 1:6; 20:4), not as Aaronic/Zadokian priests, but under Christ, who is a non-Levitical "high priest according to the order of Mel-chizedek" (Heb. 5:10; cf. Ps. 110:4). As "a priest on His throne" (Zech. 6:13), our Lord now intercedes for us night and day (Rom. 8:34; Heb. 7:25; 9:24; 1 John 2:1) against Satan, who con-stantly accuses us before God (Rev. 12:10; cf. Job 1:11; 2:5; Zech. 3:1; Luke 22:31; 1 Peter 5:8). As glorified Melchize-dekian-type priests under Christ, presumably we will repre-sent nonglorified millennial saints before God, even as Le-vitical priests represented Israel before God (Heb. 7:27), and true Christians, since Pentecost, as a "holy priesthood" (1 Peter 2:5) and a "royal priesthood" (1 Peter 2:9), pray for one another (2 Cor. 1:11; Col. 1:9; James 5:16).

(2) Righteous angels will no longer function in governmental ca-pacities.

Fallen angels, including Satan, will be confined to the Abyss (bottomless pit), presumably "the lowest part of She-ol/Hades" (Deut. 32:22) or Tartarus (2 Peter 2:4, Greek), for one thousand years (Rev. 20:1-3, 7). Thus, at last, their worst fears will be realized. At His first coming, they cried out to the Lord Jesus, "What business do we have with each other, Son of God? Have you come here to torment us before the time?" (Matt. 8:29; cf. Luke 4:34; 8:28; James 2:19). They were probably referring to the horrible fate experienced by those "angels ["the sons of God" of Gen. 6:1-4; cf. Job 1:6; 38:6-7] who abandoned their proper abode" and, since the Flood, have been confined to "pits of darkness," "in eternal bonds under darkness for the judgment of the great day" (Jude 6; 2 Peter 2:4).

The present power of Satan is due to man's rebellion against God and his (often subconscious) desire for (evil) supernatural help to lead him into deeper sin. However, the dominion over mankind that Satan and demons have exercised since the Fall will end at the Second Coming. Eve's excuse that Satan caused her to sin (Gen. 3:13) will be proven wrong. Nonglorified men will continue to sin during the millennium, not because of Satan, but because of their sin natures (James 1:14-16; cf. Rom. 7:15-25).

Righteous angels also have exercised enormous power, under God, in the world, being twice as numerous as demons (cf. Rev. 12:4). Today they watch over individual believers (Heb. 1:14; cf. Matt. 18:10) and churches (1 Cor. 11:10; cf. 1 Peter 1:12). They executed judgment during the apostolic era (Acts 12:23; cf. Matt. 26:53) and will do so during the Great Tribulation (Rev. 8, 9, 16; cf. Matt. 13:39). However, at the Second Coming, their governmental functions will be replaced by glorified saints, and they will presumably enter into a well-deserved "retirement program" (Heb. 2:5)! Through glorification, saints (in Christ) will rise to a higher level than angels, because they will participate in the judging (and rewarding?) of all angels (1 Cor. 6:3).

(3) Believers who survive the Great Tribulation will also outlive the millennium.

Seven years before the second coming of Christ, all Christian believers will have been raptured without dying (1 Cor. 15:51-52; 1 Thess. 4:17). Those Israelites and their Gentile proselytes (like Ruth the Moabitess) who will be regenerated during the Seventieth Week will in most cases be martyred (Isa. 6:13; Dan. 7:21, 25; Zech. 13:8-9; Matt. 24:9, 22; Rev. 13:15). Those believers (both Jews and Gentiles) who survive the Seventieth Week (Isa. 4:3; Zech. 14:16; Matt. 24:31; 25:31-33) will live throughout the entire millennium, thus exceeding Methuselah's amazing life span of 969 years! Not only will mortal millennial saints not die; they won't even be sick (Isa. 33:24; cf. 30:26; 35:5-6; Jer. 30:17; 33:6; Hos. 6:1). Thus, the longevity limits of Psalm 90:10 will be cancelled, and mere human schemes to greatly extend life (including "faith healing" and "genetic engineering") will be utterly discredited (see number 14 below).

(4) Jerusalem will be the religious and political center of the world.

The millennial Jerusalem will truly be a glorious city (but not to be confused with the vastly more glorious New Jerusalem of Rev. 21–22). God's WORD will go forth from there (Isa. 2:3; Zech. 8:20-23); and by responding to that message, Gentiles will be spiritually "born there" (Ps. 87:4-7). In spite of her often-tragic history, "the LORD will again choose Jerusalem" (Zech. 2:12; cf. 1:14-17; 2:1-11; 3:2; 2 Chron. 6:6; Ps. 48:1-14; 68:16; 78:76; 84:5; 132:13-14). The size and location of the city is given in Ezekiel 48:15-35. Its religious name will be not only "Zion" but also "The Lord is there" (Ezek. 48:35), as well as "The LORD our Righteousness" (Jer. 33:16), "The City of the LORD" (Isa. 60:14), and "The Throne of the LORD" (Jer. 3:17). At the end of the millennium, it will also be called "the camp of the saints and the beloved city" (Rev. 20:9).

(5) World worship will be centered at the millennial temple.[4]

A careful reading of Ezekiel 40–42 gives one the clear impression of a future literal temple for Israel because of the immense number of details concerning its dimensions, its parts, and its contents. Ezekiel was given specific instructions to "declare to the house of Israel all that you see" (40:4), which seems strange if the temple were to symbolize only general truths. Even more significant is the fact that the Israelites are to "observe its whole design and all its statutes and do them" (43:11). This is an exact parallel to the pattern of the tabernacle, which Moses saw in the Mount, and which God commanded him to construct (Exod. 25:8-9).

All will agree that the temple of Ezekiel 8–11 was the literal temple of Ezekiel's day, even though the prophet saw it "in the visions of God" (8:3) while he himself was still in Babylon (8:1). In these four chapters we find mention of "the entrance of the north gate of the inner court" (8:3), "the porch" (8:16), "the altar" (8:16), "the threshold of the temple" (9:3), and "the east gate of the Lord's house" (10:19). Now without any indication whatever that an ideal temple instead of a literal temple is being set forth in chapters 40–42, we find similar, if not identical, descriptive formulas being used: "in the visions of God" (40:2; cf. 8:3), "a gate toward the south" (40:27; cf. 8:3), "the porch of the temple" (40:48; cf. 8:16), "the altar" (43:18; cf. 8:16), and "the gate facing toward the east" (43:1; cf. 10:19), through which the glory of the God of Israel is seen returning, exactly as He had departed, according to 10:19 and 11:23. Now if the millennial temple is not to be a reality, then why insist that the return of the God of Israel is to be a reality? Ezekiel is not the only Old Testament prophet who saw a future, glori-

---

[4] See chapter 11 for full analysis of the millennial temple. For the reader's convenience, this section repeats what is found on pages 153-55.

ous temple for God's chosen people Israel (Joel 3:18; Isa. 2:3; 60:13; Dan. 9:24; Hag. 2:7, 9), complete with animal sacrifices, in the Holy Land (Isa. 56:6-7; 60:7; Jer. 33:18; Zech. 14:16-21).

God has definitely promised to the line of Zadok an everlasting priesthood (1 Sam. 2:35; 1 Kings 2:27, 35). This confirms God's promise of an everlasting priesthood to Zadok's ancestor, Phinehas (Num. 25:13), which also confirms His promise of an everlasting priesthood to Phinehas's grandfather, Aaron (Exod. 29:9; 40:15). Furthermore, this promise of an everlasting priesthood was strongly confirmed by God through Jeremiah, who links the perpetuity of the Levitical priests with the perpetuity of the Davidic kingship and the perpetuity of the earth's rotation on its axis (Jer. 33:17-22)! In view of these promises of God, confirmed again and again, it is highly significant that the millennial temple of Ezekiel will have the sons of Zakok as its priests (Ezek. 40:46; 44:15)! God apparently means what He says!

The intrinsic probability of this being fulfilled literally is strengthened tremendously by the mention of 12,000 Levites who will be sealed by God during the yet future seventieth week of Daniel (Rev. 7:7). If these are literal Levites, it would hardly be consistent to maintain that the temple is spiritual or figurative. And if God's promises to Aaron, Phinehas, and Zadok are spiritualized, how can we insist that His promises to David will be fulfilled literally (2 Sam. 7:13, 16)? The Bible clearly teaches that while there is no such thing as an earthly temple, an altar, or animal sacrifices in true Christianity (John 4:21; Heb. 7–10), there will be such provisions for Israel following the rapture of the Church (Matt. 24; 2 Thess. 2:4; Rev. 11:1-2. Compare also Hos. 3:4-5 with Dan. 9:24, 27). Furthermore, Revelation 20:9 indicates that Jerusalem, the "beloved city," will once again be "the camp of the saints" during the millennial age.

The clear New Testament teaching of a post-rapture "holy place" and "temple of God" in Jerusalem, complete with "the altar" (Rev. 11:1), prepares us to anticipate a millennial temple in connection with the "holy city" Jerusalem, in harmony with Old Testament teaching.

(6) Christ's return to earth will be followed by a 30-day cleansing period.

Within 30 days following His return, our Lord will have cleansed the temple contaminated by the Abomination of Desolation 1290 days earlier (Dan. 12:11).[5]

(7) There will be a 75-day Divine confrontation of Israelite and Gentile leaders who survive the Great Tribulation.

From the resurrection of the Antichrist (at the middle of the Seventieth Week) to the final removal of all his followers will be 1,335 days (1,260 + 75 = 1,335). Immediately following Christ's second coming to the earth and the destruction of all earthly armies at Armageddon, our Lord will inaugurate a 75-day purging process of all mankind, beginning with Israel (Ezek. 20:33-38; Mal. 3:1-6; Isa. 4:3-4; compare the three-month purge under Ezra's leadership at the Kidron Valley in Ezra 10:7-17); continuing with national leaders in "The Valley of Decision" (i.e., the Kidron Valley—Joel 3:1-17; Matt. 25:31-46); and ending with every single man and woman throughout the world at the posttribulational "rapture to judgment" (Matt. 24: 37-41; Luke 17:34-37; cf. Matt. 13:30, 41-42, 49; in contrast to the pre-Seventieth Week rapture of the true Church to glory).

God told Daniel, "How blessed is he who keeps waiting and attains to the 1,335 days!" (Dan. 12:12). This covers the time from Satan's desecration of the temple through the Abomination of Desolation to the end of the purging period 75

---

[5] For details see chapter 6, under "The 1,290 Days and the 1,335 Days."

days after the Second Coming, which, in turn, is exactly 1,260 days after the Abomination (Rev. 12:6; 13:5). By that day, the great 1,335th day, all unregenerate people will have been removed (as at the Flood); "all Israel will be saved" (Rom. 11: 26; Matt. 24:13); and all those who survive until the dawn of the millennium will be called "blessed."

(8) All saints, glorified and nonglorified, will sit with Christ in His great inaugural banquet.

Our Lord confirmed Isaiah's prophecy of an inaugural banquet for the kingdom age (Isa. 25:6), when He spoke of drinking new wine with His disciples "in my Father's kingdom" (Matt. 26:29; Luke 22:16, 18). Then, He told them, they "will recline at the table with Abraham, Isaac, and Jacob in the kingdom of heaven" (Matt. 8:11; Luke 13:28-29). How amazed survivors of the tribulation will be, to behold Christ's glorious bride, the Church!

(9) There will be a seven-month process of cleansing the land of human bones.

Seven months will be needed to bury human bones left from Gog's armies (which will be destroyed in southern Israel at the mid-point of the Seventieth Week) and from the Battle of Armageddon (in northern Israel at the end of the Seventieth Week). Following the Second Coming, regathered Israel will begin cleansing her devastated land. "For seven months the house of Israel will be burying [human skeletons] in order to cleanse the land ... If anyone sees a man's bone, then he will set up a marker by it until the buriers have buried it" (Ezek. 39:9; cf. Isa. 2:4; 9:5; cf. Hos. 2:18; Zech. 9:10).

(10) The removal of war implements will be a seven-year process.

Seven years will be needed to remove all implements of war scattered over the Holy Land. "Then those who inhabit the cities of Israel will go out, and make fires with the weapons and burn them ... and for seven years they will make fires of them" (Ezek. 39:9; cf. Isa. 2:4; 9:5; Hos. 2:18; Zech. 9:10).

(11) There will be a forty-year desolation of Egypt.

Forty years of national humiliation will be experienced by Egypt. Egypt was doubtless the most oppressive enemy Israel ever knew—with Assyria a close second (Isa. 52:4). Even though some Egyptians (and Assyrians) will trust the Messiah, presumably through Jewish witnesses during the last half of the Seventieth Week (Isa. 19:18-25; cf. Ps. 87:4-6), God will make Egypt an object lesson, during the early years of the millennium, of His anger toward those who oppress His people (Gen. 12:3). "I shall make the land of Egypt a desolation for forty years ... I shall scatter the Egyptians among the nations and disperse them among the lands ... At the end of forty years I shall gather the Egyptians from the peoples among whom they were scattered, and ... they will be the lowest of the kingdoms" (Ezek. 29:11-16).[6]

(12) The millennial government will be outwardly perfect.

As the holy and righteous Davidic King, Christ will rule the world with "a rod of iron" and will eliminate all crime, corruption, and war. At the Second Coming, all military resistance to Christ will be smashed: "You shall break them with a rod of iron, You shall shatter them like earthenware" (Ps. 2:9; cf. 110:6; Isa. 11:4; Dan. 2:34, 35, 44, 45). The "rod of iron" symbolizes His future reign as King of Kings upon the earth (Rev. 2:27; 12:5; 19:15; cf. Jer. 23:5; 33:15; Zech. 6:13; Rev. 11:15; 19:16). Only the Son of God can eliminate war, crime, and cor-

---

[6] See chapter 10 for more on the future of Egypt.

ruption in the nations and restore His once-magnificent planet (Rom. 8:21).

(13) The knowledge of the Lord will cover the entire earth, and all education will be religiously orthodox.

Under Christ the King, all arts, sciences, and education will be in harmony with revealed truth. Materialism, humanism, evolutionism, occultism, and all false religions will vanish from centers of learning. At the beginning of the kingdom, there will be no need for evangelism (Jer. 31:34), and throughout the millennium "the earth will be full of the knowledge of the Lord as the waters cover the sea" (Isa. 11:9; cf. 66:23; Zech. 14:9). Just as the personal and prolonged presence of the Lord Jesus with His disciples was essential for their spiritual maturity, so also in the kingdom deep teaching over long periods of time will be the plan of God for the progressive sanctification of His people.

(14) There will be a vast population explosion.

Only on rare occasions will people die during the kingdom age. Only a relatively small remnant of Jews and Gentiles will enter the kingdom with mortal bodies, surviving the 1,335th day (see number 7 above), even as a tiny remnant of mankind survived the Flood (Matt. 24:37-39; cf. 7:14). But at the end of the millennium, there will be multiplied billions of people, because of very long life spans, no sickness (see number 3 above), and very few deaths. Compare Exodus 1:7. In fact, the number of unbelievers by the end of the millennium will be "like the sand of the seashore" (Rev. 20:8; compare Gen. 13:16; 15:5; 22:17; 26:4; 32:12 with Deut. 1:10-11; 1 Kings 4:20).

The enormity of kingdom population growth, especially in the Holy Land, is emphasized in Isaiah 49:19-21; 54:1-2; Jeremiah 33:22; and Zechariah 8:4; 10:8, 10. Every available earthly resource will be utilized for man's survival and prosperity. Human death during the millennium will be so rare that a man dying at the age of one hundred will be considered a mere "youth." In fact, such a person will die only because he has been "cursed" by God, presumably because of open rebellion (Isa. 65:20).

(15) All people born in the millennium will still possess a sin nature.

All children born during the kingdom age, as in every age of human history (such as Cain soon after Creation, and Canaan soon after the Flood), will possess sinful natures (Pss. 51:5; 58:3; Jer. 17:9; Rom. 3:23). Most of these (as in every generation since Adam) will reject the grace of God, while paying lip service out of fear of His rod of iron (see number 12 above). Similarly, our Lord tolerated an unregenerate Judas for over three years—to such an extent that the eleven regenerate apostles did not even know that he was the betrayer (John 13:22)! As world population explodes toward the end of the millennium, potential rebellion will become volcanic. By the end, a "Judas mentality" will have so dominated the vast majority of humanity that Satan's sudden (though "for a short time") availability to them (through our Lord's permissive will, granting to men the secret desires of their hearts—Pss. 78:29; 106:15) will bring people "like the sand of the seashore" to surround and attack "the camp of the saints and the beloved city [Jerusalem]" (Rev. 20:8-9).

(16) At the end of the millennium, Satan will be released from the Abyss "for a short time" to deceive those who reject Christ as Savior.

All believing ("sheep" or "wheat") Gentiles will at first rejoice at the prospect of worshipping the God of Israel (Zech. 8). As the centuries pass, unbelieving descendants of these believers (and Jewish believers too) will increasingly dominate the world's population and will show reluctance to come to the temple to worship the King (Zech. 14). For the last time, God will use Satan to test mankind, just as He did in the Garden of Eden, to bring to light the true motives of men's hearts, "in order that those who are approved may become evident" (1 Cor. 11:19). A perfectly righteous government and wicked men cannot long coexist, for "though the wicked is shown favor [as our Lord did to Judas], he does not learn righteousness; he deals unjustly in the land of uprightness, and does not perceive the majesty of the Lord" (Isa. 26:10). Therefore, Satan "must be released for a short time" (Rev. 20:3; cf. v. 7), because he must, under God's direction, "come out [from his millennial prison] to deceive the nations that are in the four corners of the earth" (Rev. 20:7-8; see numbers 14 and 15 above). A thousand years of torment in the Abyss (see number 2 above) will not have modified his hatred for God, nor his desire to pervert those who bear His image.

Charles C. Ryrie helpfully explains:

> When the Millennium begins, people with earthly bodies will enter it, but apparently none of them will be unsaved at the very beginning. But quite soon (perhaps in the first minutes) babies will be born, and in a thousand years many children will come into the world, grow up, and live unusually long lives. All of them will be obliged to give outward allegiance to Christ ... but as in every age He will not compel them to believe in their hearts. Consequently, there will be many living who have never turned to Christ for salvation, though they have obeyed Him as Head of the government. These will seize on the chance to give expression to the rebellion of their

hearts when Satan arises to be their leader in this last revolt. The Millennium will prove, among other things, that a nearly perfect earthly environment (Isa. 35) and universal knowledge of the Lord (Isa. 11:9) will not change human hearts. This must be done personally and voluntarily, and multitudes will never do that during this long period.[7]

---

[7] Charles C. Ryrie, *Revelation*, new edition (Chicago: Moody, 1996), 134.

14

Beyond the Millennium

When the thousand-year mediatorial kingdom on earth has come to an end, the Lord Jesus will turn it over to His Father. "For He must reign until He has put all His enemies under His feet. The last enemy that will be abolished is death ... then the Son Himself will also be subjected to the One who subjected all things to Him, so that God may be all in all" (1 Cor. 15:25-26, 28).

The New Heavens and the New Earth

Then will come "a new heaven and a new earth," which will continue forever (Rev. 21:1). Peter described it as "new heavens and a new earth, in which righteousness dwells" (2 Peter 3:13). What will it be like? First, we find an amazing list of negatives: there will be no longer any sea (Rev. 21:1); there will be neither sun nor moon (21:23); and there will be no night because Christ will be the light of the world (21:23-25). For God's people there will be no more shedding of tears, for there will be no more death, or mourning, or crying, or pain, for "the first things have passed away" (21:4). In fact, "nothing unclean, and no one who practices abominations and lying, shall ever come into it" (21:27), and thus "there will no longer be any curse" (22:3).

Even more surprising, perhaps, in contrast to the thousand-year kingdom, there will be "no temple in it." Why not?

Because "the LORD God, the Almighty [the Father], and the Lamb [the Son], are its temple" (21:22). Thus, there will be no need for an altar, with priests to offer animals. How different that will be for the nation of Israel!

But what about the positive aspects of this eternal kingdom? "The New Jerusalem" will be an enormous structure, 1,500 miles long, wide, and high (21:16)! It will be surrounded by a gigantic wall made of jasper, with twelve gates named for the twelve tribes of Israel (21:12). The city will have twelve foundation stones named for the twelve apostles (essentially equivalent to the Church). Through these gates and into the city "the kings of the earth ... will bring their glory and the honor of the nations" (21:24, 26). Thus, forever the distinctive characteristics of the true Church, the redeemed nation of Israel, and the believing Gentile nations will be perpetuated.

The Great White Throne

What will happen to unbelievers who have died? Their destiny, like that of believers, will be fixed (Rev. 22:11). As our Lord explained, all unbelievers "will go away into eternal punishment, but the righteous into eternal life" (Matt. 25:46). He told us that this place of punishment, "Gehenna," will be a "Lake of Fire" that burns forever (Matt. 5:22, 29, 30; 10:28; 18:9; 23:15, 33; Mark 9:43, 45, 47; Luke 12:5; cf. Rev. 14:11; 20:10, 14). How will this be determined? When our present universe disappears, God will establish "a great white throne," before which all un-believers will stand (Rev. 20:11-12). Books will be opened, especially "the book of life," and the dead will be "judged from the things which were written in the books, according to their deeds ... And if anyone's name [is] not found written in the book of life, he [will be] thrown into the lake of fire" (Rev. 20:12, 15).

211

"It would be inconsistent to accept Christ's teachings on salvation or on ethics as authoritative but deny His assertions about eternal punishment. Those who respect Jesus Christ will believe in the existence of an eternal Lake of Fire."[1]

Four thousand years ago, God told Abraham that He was about to judge the cities of Sodom and Gomorrah—where his nephew Lot lived—for their awful depravity. Abraham had no comprehension of the magnitude of their sin, but he did know that "the Judge of all the earth" would indeed "deal justly" (Gen. 18:25). Hundreds of years later, God told the prophet Ezekiel, "'As I live!' declares the Lord GOD, 'I take no pleasure in the death of the wicked'" (Ezek. 33:11).

The Lord Jesus told us of a wealthy unbeliever who died and went to "a place of torment" called Hades (Luke 16:19-31). Amazingly, he did not call for justice! Nor did he say God was treating him unfairly. Instead, he cried out: "Father Abraham, have mercy on me." In other words, he knew he was experiencing exactly what he deserved. So will it be for all unbelievers throughout eternity. Repeatedly, our Creator tells them, "I am He who searches the minds and hearts; and I will give to each one of you according to your deeds" (Rev. 2:23; cf. Ps. 62:12; Jer. 17:10; Matt. 16:27; Rom. 2:6; Rev. 20:12-13; 22:12).

When this present world disappears, unsaved persons who have died will not be confronted by Abraham but by Christ Himself! They "will be tormented ... in the presence of the Lamb" (Rev. 14:10). They will be in the presence of the One who not only created them in His image but also died for them on the cross! He paid the awful price "for our sins; and

---

[1] Steven Waterhouse, *Not By Bread Alone: An Outlined Guide to Bible Doctrine* (Amarillo, TX: Westcliff Press, 2010), 537.

not for ours only, but also for those of the whole world" (1 John 2:2).

Friend, "there is no partiality with God" (Rom. 2:11), because "the God who inflicts wrath is not unrighteous, is He? ... May it never be! For otherwise, how will God judge the world?" (Rom. 3:5-6).

A Final Invitation

Let us accept His infinite gift of salvation and receive what we do not deserve—eternal life! Let us respond to those precious words of invitation with which the Bible ends: "The Spirit and the bride [the Church] say, 'Come.' And let the one who hears say, 'Come.' And let the one who is thirsty come; let the one who wishes take the water of life without cost. ... He who testifies to these things says, 'Yes, I am coming quickly.' Amen. Come, Lord Jesus" (Rev. 22:16-17, 20).

Author Index

Scripture Index

RESOURCE MATERIAL
ON BIBLE PROPHECY
from
Whitcomb Ministries

Books
Daniel (176 pages).. $11
Esther and the Destiny of Israel (129 pages)........................... $10
The Interpretation of Prophecy, by Paul L. Tan (437 pages) $8

DVD Courses
The Greatness of the Kingdom (16 hours)............................ $120
Biblical Eschatology (27 hours) $200

Home Bible Study Audio Albums
The Five Worlds (6 CDs)... $24
The Second Coming of Christ (6 CDs).................................... $24
The Greatest Prophecy: Isaiah 53 (4 CDs) $17
Daniel (10 CDs)... $38
Zechariah (12 CDs).. $45
Malachi (10 CDs)... $38

Bible Chronology Charts
Three plastic-coated charts on Bible prophecy......................... $7

For orders call (317) 250-5469

***

WHITCOMB MINISTRIES
10203 Coral Reef Way, Indianapolis, IN 46256

E-mail: WhitcombMinistry@gmail.com

Website: www.whitcombministries.org

Listen to archived sermons at:
www.sermonaudio.com/whitcomb

http://windowforwomen.blogspot.com

REQUEST A CATALOG

Made in the USA
Charleston, SC
01 October 2013